HOW
TO BE
A POET

Also by J. M. Farkas

Be Brave: An Unlikely Manual for Erasing Heartbreak

HOW
TO BE
A POET

J. M. Farkas

Andrews McMeel
PUBLISHING®

For my mother, Agnes, who learned to love music from her mother and then gave this love to me: Ma's lullaby taught us to sing—you taught me how to be a poet.

POETRY & MOTORCYCLES:
AN UNLIKELY INTRODUCTION

Ovid, the famed poet who is most known for writing the *Metamorphoses,* was banished from Rome in 8 CE by the decree of Emperor Augustus. He said that the cause of his exile was *carmen et error,* which translates into "a poem and an error." Some believe that this poetic mistake was the publication of Ovid's most controversial work, *Ars Amatoria*—a book you are holding in your hands right now and will soon find in an altered form.

How to Be a Poet uses Ovid's *Ars Amatoria* as the source text for erasure. *Ars Amatoria,* which means "art of love" or "textbook of love," is a series of elegiac instructions written in three parts. In the first two sections, Ovid, who considers himself a master of love, addresses young men with equal parts scandalousness and seriousness, in order to teach them how to find and keep the objects of their affection. The last section, written several years later, offers equally unabashed advice to young women or "girls" on how to, essentially, land a man.

When I came across *The Art of Love,* I was totally shocked. This ancient advice book on relationships, sex, and dating, written in 2 CE, is certainly outrageous but can be remarkably modern, fresh, and timely. It's one part literary manual and one part *Cosmopolitan* magazine. Ovid's instructions can seem both provocative and hilarious, both progressive and offensive. It's sometimes spot-on, often very sexist, and even a little X-rated.

Here are some of the startling things Ovid says when he offers his self-proclaimed "masterful" advice to young women. He believes in covering up your flaws: "hide your body's defects as best as you may. If you're short sit down . . . commit your smallness to your couch." He encourages excessive wine drinking as a means of amplifying your date's beer goggles: "Even if you're plain, with drink you'll seem beautiful, and night itself grants concealment to your failings." What at first seems like tame advice—Ovid recommends writing letters to the object of your affection—turns out to be a manipulation strategy to maintain the upper hand: "Make him fear and hope together, every time you write." Ovid is a big proponent of playing games, both recreationally (knucklebones—the ancient version of jacks!) and romantically. He sees love as a sport and espouses a very modern sensibility, in the sense of being "a player." Ovid enthusiastically suggests using jealousy, deceit, and fear to keep a man interested and to successfully woo him: "safe loving should be mixed with fright, lest he consider you hardly worth a night."

Any way you slice it, whether Ovid is loathsome or doles out relationship truth, *Ars Amatoria* is a compelling read. It was also the perfect book to "erase," because I knew that I could transform it into something completely different than what it was. I could keep the idea of an advice or how-to book but abandon everything irksome about it. Instead of teaching girls how to win over guys, I actually eliminated the guys altogether.

How to Be A Poet might sound like a manual for writing poetry, and in some ways it is. Many believe it's impossible to teach someone how to be a poet, and it's for that exact reason that some of the instructions in this book include unaccomplishable tasks. Part of the beauty of poetry, after all, is its indefinability—and sometimes its impossibility. But *How to Be a Poet* is much more expansive than what it seems. Poetry is a metaphor for many things. It's a metaphor for being an artist. It's a metaphor for girlhood. It's a metaphor for the art of being a girl. It's a metaphor for paying attention. It's a metaphor for being and seeking, for navigating this one world like a poet, which is to say with both curiosity and courage.

When I was writing this book, at times it felt like a letter to young girls. I was writing with many of my beloved former students in mind. I was writing to the girls in my creative writing classes whose work inspired me. Girls who sat in my windowless office and shared their writing and non-writing lives with me. I was writing to the little girl inside me too. To my mother. And to the little girl inside my mother. But what I never knew: I was also writing about motorcycles.

My first book, *Be Brave,* while originally about romantic heartbreak, also evolved into an unexpected elegy that honored the legacy of my late grandmother, Eva Braun, who everyone called "Ma." Her shining face is on the book's cover, and her beautiful photo and special smile wait inside the pages. At the end of the book, there is also an extended dedication. It was something I thought I was only writing for my family, but it turns out that so many readers were touched by Ma too. This is the power of my remarkable grandmother—even after she was gone, she was able to move people with her story.

So I wanted to continue this tradition of featuring amazing and brave and poetic women on the cover of my books. In a way, I see my two books of erasure as sisters. One day, I stumbled upon a photo of Anne-France Dautheville, and I humbly believed deep inside me that I had to have her on the cover of *How to Be a Poet*. As soon as I saw this astonishing picture of Anne-France in a floral dress on her motorcycle, my heart tripled in speed—the image was poetry in motion.

When I learned more about the woman in the photograph, I was even more blown away. Anne-France is a writer and a world-record holder. According to an August 15, 2016, article in the *New York Times Style Magazine,* "From 1972 to 1981, she motored across the globe: First across the Orion Raid, a motorcycle tour from Paris to Isfahan, Iran; then to Afghanistan. In 1973, she became the first woman to ride across the world solo on a motorcycle: Astride a Kawasaki 125, she trekked three continents and covered 12,500 miles." More recently, in 2016, designer Clare Waight Keller and the fashion house Chloé used Dautheville as inspiration for their collection.

You might think poetry and motorcycles don't have much in common, but Professor Google proves this wrong. Through a little research, I discovered a great blog post from November 16, 2007, on the *Guardian* website in which the writer, Shirley Dent, explains: "The motorbike and the poem are creatures akin. They straddle physical and intellectual sense—even though you feel physics working through you when you are on a bike, being on a bike is not about succumbing to the physical or losing all sense. There is precise science in the recklessness of both riding a bike and writing a poem."

★ ★ ★

What most excites me about my second book is that it's actually two books in one. The first half of *How to Be a Poet* contains my erasure of Ovid's *Ars Amatoria,* using a whiteout poetry technique. The second half reveals the full, readable text of Ovid's original work, with my "found" poem in bolded letters and embedded in the source text. This style of erasure is inspired by one of my most influential teachers, Jen Bervin, and her book *Nets,* which uses Shakespeare's sonnets as a palimpsest. This particular aesthetic gives readers a little more access and insight into my process, as well as an understanding of how radically different one text is from the other. One reason why erasure lures me is the idea of extreme possibility—that you can transform any story (even your own). Readers can also enjoy Ovid's work and come to their own conclusions about whether his advice on love is artful or artless. A quick little note on the handmade process: because there is more whimsy in my second book of erasure, I felt it needed more breath and white space and wind in the hair, so I decided to alter the blackout method. I traded in my Sharpie for actual Wite-Out. It took exactly seven bottles to create this book.

How to Be a Poet also prompted me to look back at some other female writers who have inspired me and this work. Both *Be Brave* and *How to Be a Poet* are written in imperatives, and

I started to think about when I first became so compelled by the second-person point of view. The "you" that can read like a first-person "I" but with more intimacy and by implicating the reader even more.

So when I thought about my reading history, I was drawn back into a surprising genre that I think most affected this work—not poetry but short story. There are two writers in particular whose works in second person have deeply and retrospectively affected me. *Self-Help* by Lorrie Moore is a collection of stories told in second person. Her piece "How to Become a Writer" is practically required reading in writing classes and famously begins: "First, try to be something, anything, else." Julie Orringer's *How to Breathe Underwater* also contains one of my favorite short stories of all time, called "Note to Sixth-Grade Self." In it, the narrator uses the second person to speak to her younger self. I have included this story in almost every class I have ever taught, and my students have created beautiful works using this piece as a model. I can only say that I have not been the same person or writer since I read this heartbreaking story.

★ ★ ★

When I first sent Anne-France Dautheville an e-mail, I was delighted to learn that she was just as feisty and inspiring in her writing as she was in her photo. Part of our exchange included a brief discussion of feminism, in which Anne-France offered this very unexpected and clever admission: "In fact I am not a feminist of any kind because I want men and women to go forward together. And also because I carry this huge hope to see men someday become as intelligent as women; but it is not for tomorrow." When I told her that I consider her to be a poet too, she wrote back: "Maybe I am a poet, but with grease under the nails and a size 7 wrench and screwdriver in my handbag." She also offered up her own definition of poetry. She said: "Poetry is painting the reality with the colours of your choice, as long as it does not cut you from everybody's reality."

As if I were not already enamored enough by Anne-France, she told me that when I published this book, I shouldn't send her a copy—instead, I should hand deliver it to her in France. So in the spirit of Anne-France Dautheville's generosity, I hope readers will also envision *How to Be a Poet* as an invitation. It is less a set of directions and more of a loving dare. Not just to make a poem but to behave like one. For you to be moving and surprising and attentively-reckless. To ride on an open road with an open heart. To take wild leaps and make wild associations between unlikely things. I'm inviting you to change any story that does not serve you. For you to (re)define the adventures of poetry and art and love in your own terms—and on your own terms too.

HOW
TO BE
A POET

I

how to

be

a

poet:

come as a

darke

stars

catch

the sun in

your

one

mouth

be

trouble

be

the girl

Who

is

too   beautiful.

need

nothing

become a

City

B^e

un-boy-like

a

willing

song

if you can,

lay there

in the light.

enumerate

water

to   set your nets

cicadas in summer

with unpractised hands,

seek

out

delight

hesitate

like   ice.

Hold fast to the   fish   on the hook

hollow

the ocean

kiss the

imaginary

mouths

Bring

a

   promise:

like
an

                  apple

            in
    the
        hand

speak as if you were

stone

wildly in the

woods

unhearing

many secret things,

confessing

excessive

love

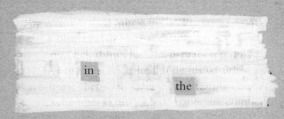

in the

fields   of

the

                              body

take what isn't given.

hope for

the

honey

 II

follow

the

sea

with

37

salt–green   lips.

hold

Violets and open lilies

39

demand

gentleness

whatever engenders

surrender

remember

43

everything

lie there on

the open roof

chase
the

heart

of

your

reader

. and

your

loveliest

rival

gather

absence

cultivate

51

your

sorrow

those
seeds

garden

are swollen with

brightness

allow

your

happiness

be seen

carry

sea-shells

in

the night

Believe me,

even

if

you

never   believed

63

Grow

a thousand

eyes

Then wait.

This is the

work.

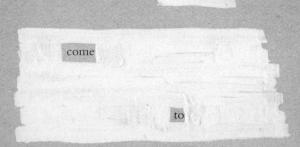

come

to

the

tender

pen

 III

Beware of the many

warnings

from your girlhood

for   example

be afraid

Be.

stubborn

75

A S

the

sky's colour,

decisive

as

teeth

forbid

your smallness

and

seek

huge

things

That suits you

I want   you

82

to

avenge your mother

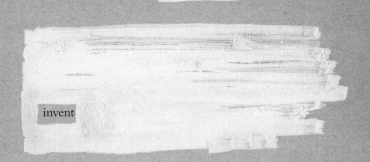

invent

a girl

with

a

reckless   heart

free

her

in her tower

be   a thief,

snatch

time

every time you write,

set   fire

to

your

arrows

of

desire

be

greedy

burn

like

A.

JEALOUS

star

.hide

the   secret

key   by

the   strawberry-trees

behind

your   heart

turn

with   the

earth

and

sing

like

a

girl

ARS AMATORIA

BOOK I

BOOK I PART I: HIS TASK

Should anyone here not know the art of love,
read this, and learn by reading **how to** love.
By art the boat's set gliding, with oar and sail,
by art the chariot's swift: love's ruled by art.
Automedon was skilled with Achilles' chariot reins,
Tiphys in Thessaly was steersman of the Argo,
Venus appointed me as guide to gentle Love:
I'll be known as Love's Tiphys, and Automedon.
It's true Love's wild, and one who often flouts me:
but he's a child of tender years, fit to be ruled.
Chiron made the young Achilles perfect at the lyre,
and tempered his wild spirits through peaceful art.
He, who so terrified his enemies and friends,
they say he greatly feared the aged Centaur.
That hand that Hector was destined to know,
was held out, at his master's orders, to **be** flogged.
I am Love's teacher as Chiron was Achilles',
both wild boys, both children of **a** goddess.
Yet the bullock's neck is bowed beneath the yoke,
and the spirited horse's teeth worn by the bit.
And Love will yield to me, though with his bow
he wounds my heart, shakes at me his burning torch.
The more he pierces me, the more violently he burns me,
so much the fitter am I to avenge the wounds.
Nor will I falsely say you gave me the art, Apollo,
no voice from a heavenly bird gives me advice,
I never caught sight of Clio or Clio's sisters
while herding the flocks, Ascra, in your valleys:
Experience prompts this work: listen to the expert **poet:**
I sing true: Venus, help my venture!

Far away from here, you badges of modesty,
the thin headband, the ankle-covering dress.
I sing of safe love, permissible intrigue,
and there'll be nothing sinful in my song.
Now the first task for you who **come as a** raw recruit
is to find out who you might wish to love.
The next task is to make sure that she likes you:
the third, to see to it that the love will last.
That's my aim, that's the ground my chariot will cover:
that's the post my thundering wheels will scrape.

BOOK I PART II: HOW TO FIND HER

While you're still free, and can roam on a loose rein,
    pick one to whom you could say: 'You alone please me.'
She won't come falling for you out of thin air:
the right girl has to be searched for: use your eyes.
The hunter knows where to spread nets for the stag,
he knows what valleys hide the angry boar:
the wild-fowler knows the woods: the fisherman
knows the waters where the most fish spawn:
You too, who search for the essence of lasting love,
must be taught the places that the girls frequent.
I don't demand you set your sails, and search,
or wear out some long road to discover them.
Perseus brought Andromeda from **dark**est India,
and Trojan Paris snatched his girl from Greece,
Rome will grant you lots of such lovely girls,
you'll say: 'Here's everything the world has had.'
Your Rome's as many girls as Gargara's sheaves,
as Methymna's grapes, as fishes in the sea,
as birds in the hidden branches, **star**s in the sky:
Venus, Aeneas's mother, haunts his city.
If you'd **catch** them very young and not yet grown,
real child-brides will come before your eyes:
if it's young girls you want, thousands will please you.
You'll be forced to be unsure of your desires:
if you delight greatly in older wiser years,
here too, believe me, there's an even greater crowd.

BOOK I PART III: SEARCH WHILE YOU'RE OUT WALKING

Just walk slowly under Pompey's shady colonnade,
when **the sun**'s **in** Leo, on the back of Hercules's lion:
or where Octavia added to her dead son Marcellus's gifts,
with those rich works of foreign marble.
Don't miss the Portico that takes its name
from Livia its creator, full of old masters:
or where the daring Danaids prepare to murder their poor husbands,
and their fierce father stands, with out-stretched sword.
And don't forget the shrine of Adonis, Venus wept for,
and the sacred Sabbath rites of the Syrian Jews.
Don't skip the Memphite temple of the linen-clad heifer:
she makes many a girl what she herself was to Jove.
And the law-courts (who'd believe it?) they suit love:
a flame is often found in the noisy courts:
where the Appian waters pulse into the air,
from under Venus's temple, made of marble,
there the lawyer's often caught by love,
and he who guides others, fails to guide himself:
in that place of eloquence often his words desert him,
and a new case starts, his own cause is the brief.
There Venus, from her neighbouring temples, laughs:
he, who was once the counsel, now wants to be the client.

BOOK I PART IV: OR AT THE THEATRE

But hunt for them, especially, at the tiered theatre:
that place is the most fruitful for **your** needs.
There you'll find one to love, or one you can play with,
one to be with just once, or **one** you might wish to keep.
As ants return home often in long processions,
carrying their favourite food in their **mouth**s,
or as the bees buzz through the flowers and thyme,
among their pastures and fragrant chosen meadows,
so our fashionable ladies crowd to the famous shows:
my choice is often constrained by such richness.
They come to see, they come to **be** seen as well:
the place is fatal to chaste modesty.
These shows were first made **trouble**some by Romulus,
when the raped Sabines delighted unmarried men.
Then no awnings hung from the marble theatre,
the stage wasn't stained with saffron perfumes:
Then what the shady Palatine provided, leaves
simply placed, was all the artless scene:
The audience sat on tiers made from turf,
and covered their shaggy hair, as **be**st they could, with leaves.
They watched, and each with his eye observed **the girl**
he wanted, and trembled greatly in his silent heart.
While, to the measure of the homely Etruscan flute,
the dancer, with triple beat, struck the levelled earth,
amongst the applause (applause that was never artful then)
the king gave the watched-for signal for the rape.
They sprang up straightaway, showing their intent by shouting,
and eagerly took possession of the women.
As doves flee the eagle, in a frightened crowd,
as the new-born lamb runs from the hostile wolf:

so they fled in panic from the lawless men,
and not one showed the colour she had before.
Now they all fear as one, but not with one face of fear:
Some tear their hair: some sit there, all will lost:
one mourns silently, another cries for her mother in vain:
one moans, one faints: one stays, while that one runs:
the captive girls were led away, a joyful prize,
and many made even fear itself look fitting.
Whoever showed too much fight, and denied her lover,
he held her clasped high to h**is** loving heart,
and said to her: 'Why mar your tender cheeks with tears?
as your father to your mother, I'll be to you.'
Romulus, alone, knew what was fitting for soldiers:
I'll be a soldier, if you give me what suits me.
From that I suppose came the theatres' usual customs:
now **too** they remain a snare for the **beautiful.**

BOOK I PART V: OR AT THE RACES, OR THE CIRCUS

Don't forget the races, those noble stallions:
the Circus holds room for a vast obliging crowd.
No **need** here for fingers to give secret messages,
nor a nod of the head to tell you she accepts:
You can sit by your lady: **nothing**'s forbidden,
press your thigh to hers, as you can do, all the time:
and it's good the rows force you close, even if you don't like it,
since the girl is touched through the rules of the place.
Now find your reason for friendly conversation,
and first of all engage in casual talk.
Make earnest enquiry whose those horses are:
and rush to back her favourite, whatever it is.
When the crowded procession of ivory gods goes by,
you clap fervently for Lady Venus:
if by chance a speck of dust falls in the girl's lap,
as it may, let it be flicked away by your fingers:
and if there's nothing, flick away the nothing:
let anything be a reason for you to serve her.
If her skirt is trailing too near the ground,
lift it, and raise it carefully from the dusty earth:
Straightaway, the prize for service, if she allows it,
is that your eyes catch a glimpse of her legs.
Don't forget to look at who's sitting behind you,
that he doesn't press her sweet back with his knee.
Small things please light minds: it's very helpful
to puff up her cushion with a dextrous touch.
And it's good to raise a breeze with a light fan,
and set a hollow stool beneath her tender feet.
And the Circus brings assistance to new love,
and the scattered sand of the gladiator's ring.

Venus' boy often fights in that sand,
and who see wounds, themselves receive a wound.
While talking, touching hands, checking the programme,
and asking, having bet, which one will win,
wounded he groans, and feels the winged dart,
and himself **become**s **a** part of the show he sees.
When, lately, Caesar, in mock naval battle,
exhibited the Greek and Persian fleets,
surely young men and girls came from either coast,
and all the peoples of the world were in the **City**?
Who did not find one he might love in that crowd?
Ah, how many were tortured by an alien love!

BOOK I PART VI: TRIUMPHS ARE GOOD TOO!

Behold, now Caesar's planning to add to our rule
what's left of earth: now the far East will be ours.
Parthia, we'll have vengeance: Crassus's bust will cheer,
and those standards wickedly laid low by barbarians.
The avenger's here, the leader, proclaimed, of tender years,
and a boy wages war's **un-boy-like** agenda.
Cowards, don't count the birthdays of the gods:
a Caesar's courage flowers before its time.
Divine genius grows faster than its years,
and suffers as harmful evils the cowardly delays.
Hercules was a child when he crushed two serpents
in both his hands, already worthy of Jupiter in his cradle.
How old were you, Bacchus, who are still a boy,
when conquered India trembled to your rod?
Your father's years and powers arm you, boy,
and with your father's powers **a**nd years you'll win:
though your first beginnings must be in debt to such a name,
now prince of the young, but one day prince of the old:
Your brothers are with you, avenge your brothers' wounds:
your father is with you, keep your father's laws.
Your and your country's father endowed you with arms:
the enemy stole his kingship from an un**willing** parent:
You hold a pious shaft, he a wicked arrow:
Justice and piety stick to your standard.
Let Parthia's cause be lost: and their armies:
let my leader add Eastern wealth to Latium.
Both your fathers, Mars and Caesar, grant you power:
Through you one is a god, and one will be.
See, I augur your triumph: I'll reply with a votive **song**,
and you'll be greatly celebrated on my lips.

You'll stand and exhort your troops with my words:
O let my words not lack your courage!
I'll speak of Parthian backs and Roman fronts,
and shafts the enemy hurl from flying horses.
If you flee, to win, Parthia, what's left for you in defeat?
Mars already has your evil eye.
So the day will be, when you, beautiful one,
golden, will go by, drawn by four snowy horses.
The generals will go before you, necks weighed down with chains,
lest they flee to safety as they did before.
The happy crowd of youths and girls will watch,
that day will gladden every heart.
And if she, among them, asks the name of a king,
what place, what mountains, and what stream's displayed,
you can reply to all, and more if she asks:
and what you don't know, reply as memory prompts.
That's Euphrates, his brow crowned with reeds:
that'll be Tigris with the long green hair.
I make those Armenians, that's Persia's Danaan crown:
that was a town in the hills of Achaemenia.
Him and him, they're generals: and say what names they have,
if you can, the true ones, if not the most fitting.

BOOK I PART VII: THERE'S ALWAYS THE DINNER-TABLE

The table laid for a feast also gives you an opening:
   There's something more than wine you can look for there.
Often rosy Love has clasped Bacchus's horns,
drawing him to his gentle arms, as he **lay there**.
And when wine has soaked Cupid's drunken wings,
he's stayed, weighed down, a captive of the place.
It's true he quickly shakes out his damp feathers:
though still the heart that's sprinkled by love is hurt.
Wine rouses courage and is fit for passion:
care flies, and deep drinking dilutes it.
Then laughter comes, the poor man dons the horns,
then pain and sorrow leave, and wrinkled brows.
Then what's rarest in our age appears to our minds,
Simplicity: all art dispelled by the god.
Often at that time girls captivated men's wits,
and Venus was in the vine, flame in the fire.
Don't trust the treacherous lamplight overmuch:
night and wine can harm your view of beauty.
Paris saw the goddesses in the light, a cloudless heaven,
when he said to Venus: 'Venus, you win, over them both.'
Faults are hidden at night: every blemish is forgiven,
and the hour makes whichever girl you like beautiful.
Judge jewellery, and fabric stained with purple,
judge a face, or a figure, **in the light.**

BOOK I PART VIII: AND FINALLY THERE'S THE BEACH

Why **enumerate** every female meeting place fit for the hunter?
The grains of sand give way before the number.
Why speak of Baiae, its shore splendid with sails,
where the **water**s steam with sulphurous heat?
Here one returning, his heart wounded, said:
'That water's not as healthy as they claim.'
Behold the suburban woodland temple of Diana,
and the kingdom murder rules with guilty hand.
She, who is virgin, who hates Cupid's darts,
gives people many wounds, has many to give.

BOOK I PART IX: HOW TO WIN HER

So far, riding her unequal wheels, the Muse has taught you
where you might choose your love, where to **set your nets**.
Now I'll undertake **to** tell you what pleases her,
by what arts she's caught, itself a work of highest art.
Whoever you are, lovers everywhere, attend, with humble minds,
and you, masses, show you support me: use your thumbs.
First let faith enter into your mind: every one of them
can be won: you'll win her, if you only set your snares.
Birds will sooner be silent in the Spring, **cicadas in summer**,
an Arcadian hound turn his back on a hare,
than a woman refuse a young man's flattering words:
Even she you might think dislikes it, will like it.
Secret love's just as pleasing to women as men.
Men pretend badly: she hides her desire.
If it was proper for men not to be the first to ask,
woman's role would be to take the part of the asker.
The cow lows to the bull in gentle pastures:
the mare whinnies to the hoofed stallion.
Desire in us is milder and less frantic:
the male fire has its lawful limits.
Remember Byblis, who burned with incestuous love,
for her brother, and bravely punished herself with the noose?
Myrrha loved her father, but not as a daughter should,
and then was hidden by the covering bark:
oozing those tears, that pour from the tree as fragrance,
and whose droplets take their name from the girl.
Once, in the shady valleys of wooded Ida
there was a white bull, glory of the herd,
one small black mark set between his horns:
it the sole blemish, the rest was milky-white.

The heifers of Cnossos and Cydon longed
to have him mount up on their backs.
Pasiphae joyed in adultery with the bull:
she hated the handsome heifers with jealousy.
I sing what is well-known: not even Crete, the hundred-citied,
can deny it, however much Cretans lie.
They say that, **with unpractised hands,** she plucked
fresh leaves and tenderest grasses for the bull.
She went as one of the herd, unhindered by any care
for that husband of hers: Minos was ousted by a bull.
Why put on your finest clothes, Pasiphae?
Your lover can appreciate none of your wealth.
Why have a mirror with you, when you **seek** highland cattle?
Why continually smooth your hair, you foolish woman?
But believe the mirror that denies you're a heifer.
How you wish that brow of yours could bear horns!
If you'd please Minos, don't seek **out** adulterers:
If you want to cheat your husband, cheat with a man!
The queen left her marriage bed for woods and fields,
like a Maenad roused by the Boeotian god, they say.
Ah, how often, with angry face, she spied a cow,
and said: 'Now, how can she please my lord?
Look, how she frisks before him in the tender grass:
doubtless the foolish thing thinks that she's lovely.'
She spoke, and straightaway had her led from the vast herd,
the innocent thing dragged under the arching yoke,
or felled before the altar, forced to be a false sacrifice,
and, **delight**ed, held her rival's entrails in her hand.
The number of times she killed rivals to please the gods,
and said, holding the entrails: 'Go, and please him for me!'
Now she claims to be Io, and now Europa,
one who's a heifer, the other borne by the bull.
Yet he filled her, the king of the herd, deceived
by a wooden cow, and their offspring betrayed its breeding.
If Cretan Aerope had spurned Thyestes's love

123

(and isn't it hard to forego even one man?),
the Sun would not have veered from his course mid-way,
and turned back his chariot and horses towards Dawn.
The daughter who savaged Nisus's purple lock
presses rabid dogs down with her thighs and groin.
Agamemnon who escaped Mars on land, Neptune at sea,
became the victim of his murderous wife.
Who would not weep at Corinthian Creusa's flames,
and that mother bloodstained by her children's murder?
Phoenix, Amyntor's son wept out of sightless eyes:
Hippolytus was torn by his fear-maddened horses.
Phineus, why blind your innocent sons?
That punishment will return on your own head.
All these things were driven by woman's lust:
it's more fierce than ours, and more frenzied.
So, on, and never **hesitate** in hoping for any woman:
there's hardly one among them who'll deny you.
Whether they give or not, they're delighted to be asked:
And even if you fail, you'll escape unharmed.
But why fail, when there's pleasure in new delights
and the more foreign the more they capture the heart?
The seed's often more fertile in foreign fields,
and a neighbour's herd always has richer milk.

BOOK I PART X: FIRST SECURE THE MAID

But to get to know your desired-one's maid
is your first care: she'll smooth your way.
See if she's close to her mistress's thoughts,
and has plenty of true knowledge of her secret jests.
Corrupt her with promises, and with prayers:
you'll easily get what you want, if she wishes.
She'll tell the time (the doctors would know it too)
when her mistress's mind is receptive, fit for love.
Her mind will be fit for love when she luxuriates
in fertility, like the crop on some rich soil.
When hearts are glad, and nothing sad constrains them,
they're open: Venus steals in then with seductive art.
So Troy was defended with sorrowful conflict:
in joy, the Horse, pregnant with soldiers, was received.
She's also to be tried when she's wounded, pained by a rival:
make it your task then to see that she's avenged.
The maid can rouse her, when she combs her hair in the morning,
and add her oar to the work of your sails,
and, sighing to herself in a low murmur, say:
'But I doubt that you'll be able to make her pay.'
Then she should speak of you, and add persuasive words,
and swear you're dying, crazed with love.
But hurry, lest the sails fall and the breeze dies:
anger melts away, with time, **like** fragile **ice.**
You ask perhaps if one should take the maid herself?
Such a plan brings the greatest risk with it.
In one case, fresh from bed, she'll get busy, in another be tardy,
in one case you're a prize for her mistress, in the other herself.
There's chance in it: even if it favours the idea,
my advice nevertheless is to abstain.

I don't pick my way over sharp peaks and precipices,
no youth will be caught out being lead by me.
Still, while she's giving and taking messages,
if her body pleases you as much as her zeal,
make the lady your first priority, her companion the next:
Love should never be begun with a servant.
I warn you of this, if art's skill is to be believed,
and don't let the wind blow my words out to sea:
follow the thing through or don't attempt it:
she'll endure the whispers once she's guilty herself.
It's no help if the bird escapes when its wings are limed:
it's no good if the boar gets free from a loosened net.
Hold fast to the stricken **fish** you've caught **on the hook**:
press home the attempt, don't leave off till you've won.
She'll not give you away, sharing the guilt for the crime,
and you'll know whatever your lady's done, and said.
But hide it well: if the informer's well hidden,
you'll always secretly know your mistress's mind.

BOOK I PART XI: DON'T FORGET HER BIRTHDAY!

It's a mistake to think that only farmers working the fields,
and sailors, need to keep an eye on the season:
Seed can't always be trusted to the furrow,
or a **hollow** ship to the wine-dark sea,
It's not always safe to capture tender girls:
often the time itself makes for success.
If her birthday's here, or the April Kalends,
that delight in joining months, Venus's to Mars,
or if the Circus is decorated, not as before
with clay figurines but with the wealth of kings,
delay the thing: then winter's harsh, the Pleiades are here,
then the tender Kid is merged with **the ocean** wave:
it's best to hold off then: then he who trusts the deep,
can scarcely save the wreckage of his mangled boat.
It's fine to start on that day of tears when the Allia
flowed with the blood poured from Roman wounds,
or when the Sabbath day returns, the holy day
of the Syrian Jews, less suitable for buying things.
Let your mistress's birthday be one of great terror to you:
that's a black day when anything has to be given.
However much you avoid it, she'll still win: it's
a woman's skill, to strip wealth from an ardent lover.
A loose-robed pedlar comes to your lady: she likes to buy:
and explains his prices while you're sitting there.
She'll ask you to look, because you know what to look for:
then **kiss** you: **the**n ask you to buy her something there.
She swears that she'll be happy with it, for years,
but she needs it now, now the price is right.
If you say you haven't the money in the house, she'll ask
for a note of hand – and you're sorry you learnt to write.

Why – she asks doesn't she for money as if it's her birthday,
just for the cake, and how often it is her birthday, if she's in need?
Why – she weeps doesn't she, mournfully, for a sham loss,
that **imaginary** gem that fell from her pierced ear?
They many times ask for gifts, they never give in return:
you lose, and you'll get no thanks for your loss.
And ten **mouth**s with as many tongues wouldn't be enough
for me to describe the wicked tricks of whores.

BOOK I PART XII: WRITE AND MAKE PROMISES

Try wax to pave the way, pour it out on scraped tablets:
  let wax be your mind's true confidante.
Bring her your flattering words and play the lover:
and, whoever you are, add a humble prayer.
Achilles was moved by prayer to grant Hector's body to Priam:
a god's anger's deflected by the voice of prayer.
Make **promise**s: what harm can a promise do?
Anyone can be rich in promises.
Hope lasts, if she's once believed in,
a useful, though deceptive, goddess.
If you've given, you can quite reasonably be forgotten:
she carried it off, and now she's nothing to lose.
But if you don't give, always appear about to:
like barren fields that always cheat the farmer,
like the gambler who goes on losing, lest he's finally lost,
and calls the dice back endlessly into his eager hand.
This is the work, the labour, to have her without giving first:
and she'll go on giving, lest she lose what she's freely given.
So go on, and send your letter's flattering words,
try her intention, test the road out first.
Cydippe was deceived by the message the **apple** brought,
and unaware the girl by her own words was caught.
I warn you, youths of Rome, learn the noble arts,
not just to defend some trembl**in**g client:
like the crowd, **the** grave judge, the elected senate,
a woman will give her **hand**, won by eloquence.
But let your powers be hidden, don't display your eloquence:
let irksome words vanish from your speech.
Who, but a mindless fool, declaims to his sweet friend?
A strong letter often causes her displeasure.

Let your speech be credible, use ordinary words,
flattering though, **speak as if you were** present.
If she won't receive the letter, returns it un-read,
stick to your plan, and hope she'll read it later.
In time stubborn oxen come to the plough,
in time the horse learns to suffer the bridle:
constant use wears away an iron ring,
the curved plough's lost to the endless furrow.
What's harder than **stone**, softer than water?
Yet soft water carves the hardest stone.
Once steadfast you'll conquer Penelope herself in time:
you'll see Troy captive, though it's captured late.
She reads and won't reply? Don't press her:
just let her keep on reading your flattery.
If she wants to read, she'll want to answer what she's read:
such things proceed by number and by measure.
Perhaps at first a cool letter comes to you,
asking: would you please not trouble her.
What she asks, she fears: what she doesn't ask, she wants,
that you go on: do it, and you'll soon get what you wish.

BOOK I PART XIII: BE WHERE SHE IS

Meanwhile, if she's being carried, reclining on her bed,
secretly approach your lady's litter,
and to avoid offering your words to odious ears,
hide what you can with skill and ambiguous gestures.
If she's wandering at leisure in the spacious Colonnade,
you join here there also, lingering, as a friend:
now make as if to lead the way, now drop behind,
now **go** on quickly, and now take it slow:
don't be ashamed to slip amongst the columns,
a while, then move along side by side:
don't let her sit all beautiful in the theatre row without you:
what you'll look at is the way she holds her arms.
Gaze at her, to admire her is fine:
and to speak with gestures and with glances.
And applaud, the man who dances the girl's part:
and favour anyone who plays a lover.
When she rises, rise: while she's sitting, sit:
pass the time at your lady's whim.

BOOK I PART XIV: LOOK PRESENTABLE

Don't delight in curling your hair with tongs,
don't smooth your legs with sharp pumice stone.
Leave that to those who celebrate Cybele the Mother,
howling **wildly in the** Phrygian manner.
Male beauty's better for neglect: Theseus
carried off Ariadne, without a single pin in his hair.
Phaedra loved Hippolytus: he was unsophisticated:
Adonis was dear to the goddess, and fit for the **woods**.
Neatness pleases, a body tanned from exercise:
a well fitting and spotless toga's good:
no stiff shoe-thongs, your buckles free of rust,
no sloppy feet for you, swimming in loose hide:
don't mar your neat hair with an evil haircut:
let an expert hand trim your head and beard.
And no long nails, and make sure they're dirt-free:
and no hairs please, sprouting from your nostrils.
No bad breath exhaled from unwholesome mouth:
don't offend the nose like a herdsman or his flock.
Leave the rest for impudent women to do,
or whoever's the sort of man who needs a man.

BOOK I PART XV: AT DINNER BE BOLD

Ah, Bacchus calls to his poet: he helps lovers too,
and supports the fire with which he is inflamed.
The frantic Cretan girl wandered the unknown sands,
that the waters of tiny sea-borne Dia showed.
Just as she was, from sleep, veiled by her loose robe,
barefoot, with her yellow hair unbound,
she called, for cruel Theseus, to the **unhearing** waves,
her gentle cheeks wet with tears of shame.
She called, and wept as well, but both became her,
she was made no less beautiful by her tears.
Now striking her sweet breast with her hands, again and again,
she cried: 'That faithless man's gone: what of me, now?
What will happen to me?' she cried: and the whole shore
echoed to the sound of cymbals and frenzied drums.
She fainted in terror, her next words were stifled:
no sign of blood in her almost lifeless body.
Behold! The Bacchantes with loose streaming hair:
Behold! The wanton Satyrs, a crowd before the god:
Behold! Old Silenus, barely astride his swaybacked mule,
clutching tightly to its mane in front.
While he pursues the Bacchae, the Bacchae flee and return,
as the rascal urges the mount on with his staff.
He slips from his long-eared mule and falls headfirst:
the Satyrs cry: 'Rise again, father, rise,'
Now the God in his chariot, wreathed with vines,
curbing his team of tigers, with golden reins:
the girl's voice and colour and Theseus all lost:
three times she tried to run, three times fear held her back.
She shook, like a slender stalk of wheat stirred by the wind,
and trembled like a light reed in a marshy pool.

To whom the god said: 'See, I come, more faithful in love:
have no fear: Cretan, you'll be bride to Bacchus.
Take the heavens for dowry: be seen as heavenly stars:
and guide the anxious sailor often to your Cretan Crown.'
He spoke, and leapt from the chariot, lest she feared
his tigers: the sand yielded under his feet:
clasped in his arms (she had no power to struggle),
he carried her away: all's easily possible to a god.
Some sing 'O Hymenaeus', some 'Bacchus, euhoe!'
So on the sacred bed the god and his bride meet.
When Bacchus's gifts are set before you then,
and you find a girl sharing your couch,
pray to the father of feasts and nocturnal rites
to command the wine to bring your head no harm.
It's alright here to speak **many secret things,**
with hidden words she'll feel were spoken for her alone:
and write sweet nothings in the film of wine,
so your girl can read them herself on the table:
and gaze in her eyes with eyes **confessing** fire:
you should often have silent words and speaking face.
Be the first to snatch the cup that touched her lips,
and where she drank from, that is where you drink:
and whatever food her fingers touch, take that,
and as you take it, touch hers with your hand.
Let it be your wish besides to please the girl's husband:
it'll be more useful to you to make friends.
If you cast lots for drinking, give him the better draw:
give him the garland you were crowned with.
Though he's below you or beside you, let him always be served first:
don't hesitate to second whatever he says.
It's a safe well-trodden path to deceive in a friend's name,
though it's a safe well-trodden path, it's a crime.
That way the procurer procures far too much,
and reckons to see to more than he was charged with.
You'll be given sure limits for drinking by me:

so pay attention to your mind and feet.
Most of all beware of starting a drunken squabble,
and fists far too ready for a rough fight.
Eurytion the Centaur died, made foolish by the wine:
food and drink are fitter for sweet jests.
If you've a voice, sing: if your limbs are supple, dance:
and please, with whatever you do that's pleasing.
And though drunkenness is harmful, it's useful to pretend:
make your sly tongue stammer with lisping sounds,
then, whatever you say or do that seems too forward,
it will be thought **excessive** wine's to blame.
And speak well of your lady, speak well of the one she sleeps with:
but silently in your thoughts wish the man ill.
Then when the table's cleared, the guests are free,
the throng will give you access to her and room.
Join the crowd, and softly approach her,
let fingers brush her thigh, and foot touch foot.
Now's the time to speak to her: boorish modesty
fly far from here: Chance and Venus help the daring.
Not from my rules your eloquence will come:
desire her enough, you'll be fluent yourself.
Your's to play the lover, imitate wounds with words:
use whatever skill you have to win her belief.
Don't think it's hard: each think's herself desired:
the very worst take's pleasure in her looks.
Yet often the imitator begins to **love** in truth,
often, what was once imagined comes to be.
O, be kinder to the ones who feign it, girls:
true love will come, out of what was false.
Now secretly surprise her mind with flatteries,
as clear water undermines the hanging bank.
Never weary of praising her face, her hair,
her elegant fingers, and her slender feet.
Even the chaste like their beauty to be commended:
her form to even the virgin's pleasing and dear.

Why is losing the contest in the Phrygian woods
a cause of shame to Juno and Pallas still?
Juno's peacock shows his much-praised plumage:
if you watch **in** silence, he'll hide his wealth again.
Race-horses between races on **the** testing course,
love it when necks are patted, manes are combed.

BOOK I PART XVI: PROMISE AND DECEIVE

Don't be shy of promising: promises entice girls:
add any gods you like as witness to what you swear.
Jupiter on high laughs at lovers' perjuries,
and orders Aeolus's winds to carry them into the void.
Jupiter used to swear by the Styx, falsely, to Juno:
now he looks favourably on his own example.
Gods are useful: as they're useful, let's think they're there:
take wine and incense to the ancient altars:
indifferent calm and it's like, apathy, don't chain them:
live innocently: the divine is close at hand:
pay what you owe, hold dutifully to agreements:
commit no fraud: let your hands be free from blood.
Delude only women, if you're wise, with impunity:
where truth's more to be guarded against than fraud.
Deceive deceivers: for the most part an impious tribe:
let them fall themselves into the traps they've set.
They say in Egypt the life-giving waters failed
in the **fields**: and there were nine years **of** drought,
then Thrasius came to Busiris, and said that Jove
might be propitiated by shedding a stranger's blood.
Busiris told him: 'You become Jove's first victim,
and you be **the** stranger to give Egypt water.'
And Phalaris roasted impetuous Perillus's **body**
in the brazen bull: the unhappy creator was first to fill his work.
Both cases were just: for there's no fairer law
than that the murderous maker should perish by his art.
As liars by liars are rightfully deceived,
wounded by their own example, let women grieve.

BOOK I PART XVII: TEARS, KISSES, AND TAKE THE LEAD

And tears help: tears will move a stone:
let her see your damp cheeks if you can.
If tears (they don't always come at the right time)
fail you, touch your eyes with a wet hand.
What wise man doesn't mingle tears with kisses?
Though she might not give, **take what isn't given.**
Perhaps she'll struggle, and then say 'you're wicked':
struggling she still wants, herself, to be conquered.
Only, take care her lips aren't bruised by snatching,
and that she can't complain that you were harsh.
Who takes a kiss, and doesn't take the rest,
deserves to lose all that were granted too.
How much short of your wish are you after that kiss?
Ah me, that was boorishness stopped you not modesty.
Though you call it force: it's force that pleases girls: what delights
is often to have given what they wanted, against their will.
She who is taken in love's sudden onslaught
is pleased, and finds wickedness is a tribute.
And she who might have been forced, and escapes unscathed,
will be saddened, though her face pretends delight.
Phoebe was taken by force: force was offered her sister:
and both, when raped, were pleased with those who raped them.
Though the tale's known, it's still worth repeating,
how the girl of Scyros mated Achilles the hero.
Now the lovely goddess had given her fatal bribe
to defeat the other two beneath Ida's slopes:
now a daughter-in-law had come to Priam
from an enemy land: a Greek wife in Trojan walls:
all swore the prescribed oath to the injured husband:
now one man's grief became a nation's cause.

Shamefully, though he gave way to a mother's prayer,
Achilles hid his manhood in women's clothes.
What's this, Aeacides? Spinning's not your work:
your search for fame's through Pallas's other arts.
Why the basket? Your arm's meant to bear a shield:
why does the hand that will slay Hector hold the yarn?
Throw away the spindle wound laboriously with thread!
The spear from Pelion's to be brandished by this hand.
By chance a royal virgin shared the room:
through her rape she learned he was a man.
That she was truly won by force, we must think:
but she still wanted to be won by force.
She often cried: 'Stop!' afterwards, when Achilles hurried on:
now he'd taken up stronger weapons than the distaff.
Where's that force now? Why do you restrain
the perpetrator of your rape, Deidamia?
No doubt as there's a sort of shame in having started first,
so it's pleasant to have what someone else has started.
Ah! The youth has too much faith in his own beauty,
if he waits until she asks him first.
The man must approach first: speak the words of entreaty:
she courteously receives his flattering prayers.
To win her, ask her: she only wants to be asked:
give her the cause and the beginning of your longing.
Jupiter went as a suppliant to the heroines of old:
no woman ever seduced great Jupiter.
If you find she disdains the advent of your prayerful sighs,
leave off what you've begun, retrace your steps.
What shuns them, they desire the more: they hate what's there:
remove her loathing by pursuing less.
The **hope**d-**for** love should not always be declared:
introduce desire hidden in the name of friendship.
I've seen the most severe of women fooled this way:
he who once was a worshipper, became a lover.

BOOK I PART XVIII: BE PALE: BE WARY OF YOUR FRIENDS

A pale colour would shame a sailor on the ocean wave,
who's blackened by the rays of the sun:
and shame the farmer who turns the soil with curved plough
and heavy harrow, underneath the heavens.
And you who seek the athlete's crown, you too
would be ashamed if all your body was white.
Let all lovers be pale: it's **the** colour fitting for love:
it suits, though fools have thought it of no value.
Orion wandered pale, for Side, in the woods,
Daphnis was pale for his reluctant Naiad.
Let your leanness show your heart: don't think it a shame
to slip a cape over your shining hair:
Let youthful limbs be worn away by sleepless nights
and care, and the grief of a great love.
To gain your desire, be miserable,
and those who see you can say 'You're in love.'
Should I lament, warn you perhaps that right and wrong
are confused by all? Friendship and loyalty empty words.
Ah me, it's not safe to praise your love to a friend:
if he believes your praise, he'll steal her himself.
But Patroclus never disgraced Achilles's bed:
and how modest Phaedra was with Pirithous.
Pylades loved Hermione, just as Phoebus Pallas,
or as Castor was twin to you Pollux.
Who hopes for that, hopes for apple-bearing tamarisks,
and looks for **honey** in the middle of the stream.
All delight in what's shameful: care only for their pleasures,
and are pleased too when trouble comes to others.
Ah it's a crime! It's not their rivals that lovers fear:
flee those you think are friends, and you'll be safe.

Beware of brothers, relatives, and dear friends:
that crowd offers you true cause for fear.

BOOK I PART XIX: BE FLEXIBLE

I've done, but there's diversity in women's
hearts: a thousand minds require a thousand methods.
One soil doesn't bear all crops: vines here
are good, olives there: this teems with healthy wheat.
There are as many manners of heart as kinds of face:
a wise man will adapt to many forms,
and like Proteus now, melt into the smooth waters,
now be a tree, now a lion, now a bristling boar.
These fish are speared, those caught on a hook:
others trawled in billowing nets with straining ropes.
One mode won't suit you for every age-group:
the older hinds spot a trap from further off.
If the simple find you cunning, and the modest crude,
the poor things will straightaway mistrust themselves.
So it happens that she who fears to trust an honest man,
falls to the embrace of some low rascal.
Part of my task is left: part of the labour's done.
Moor my boat here to the anchor-chains.

BOOK II

BOOK II PART I: HIS TASK

Sing out the Paean: sing out the Paean twice!
The prize I searched for falls into my net.
Delighted lovers grant my songs the palm,
I'm preferred to Hesiod and old Homer.
So Paris the stranger sailed, from hostile Amyclae's shore,
under white sheets, with his ravished bride:
such was Pelops who brought you home Hippodamia,
borne on the foreign wheels of his conquering car.
What's your hurry, young man? Your boat's mid ocean,
and the harbour I search for is far away.
It's not enough the girl's come to you, through me, the poet:
she's captured by my art, she's to be kept by my art too.
There's no less virtue in keeping than in finding.
There's chance in the latter: the first's a work of art.
Now aid me, your **follow**er, Venus, and the Boy,
and Erato, Muse, now you have love's name too.
Great my task as I try to tell what arts can make Love stay:
that boy who wanders so, through the vast world.
And he's flighty, and has two wings on which he vanishes:
it's a tricky job to pin him down.
Minos blocked every road of flight for his guest:
but Daedalus devised a bold winged path.
When he'd imprisoned the offspring of its mother's sin,
the man half-bull, the bull who was half-man,
he said: 'Minos, the Just, let my exile end:
let my native land receive my ashes.
And since I couldn't live in my own country,
driven from it by cruel fate, still let me die there.
Give my boy freedom, if the father's service was worthless:
or if power will not spare the child, let it spare the old.'

He spoke the words, but they, and so many others, were in vain:
his freedom was still denied him by **the** king.
When he realised this, he said: 'Now, now, O Daedalus,
you have an object for your skilfulness.
Minos rules the earth and the waves:
neither land or **sea** is open for my flight.
The sky road still remains: we'll try the heavens.
Jupiter, on high, favour my plan:
I don't aspire to touch the starry spheres:
there is no way to flee the king but this.
I'd swim the Stygian waves, if Styx offered me a path:
through my nature new laws are mine.'
Trouble often sharpens the wits: who would think
any man could travel by the air-roads?
He lays out oar-like wings with lines of feathers,
and ties the fragile work with fastenings of string,
and glues the ends with beeswax melted in the flames,
and now the work of this new art's complete.
Laughing, his son handled the wax and feathers
not knowing they were being readied for his own shoulders.
His father said of them: 'This is the art that will take us home,
by this creation we'll escape from Minos.
Minos bars all other ways but cannot close the skies:
as is fitting, my invention cleaves the air.
But don't gaze at the Bear, that Arcadian girl,
or Bootes's companion, Orion **with** his sword:
Fly behind me with the wings I give you: I'll go in front:
your job's to follow: you'll be safe where I lead.
For if we go near the sun through the airy aether,
the wax will not endure the heat:
if our humble wings glide close to ocean,
the breaking salt waves will drench our feathers.
Fly between the two: and fear the breeze as well,
spread your wings and follow, as the winds allow.'
As he warns, he fits the wings to his child, shows

how they move, as a bird teaches her young nestlings.
Then he fastened the wings he'd fashioned to his own shoulders,
and poised his anxious body for the strange path.
Now, about to fly, he gave the small boy a kiss,
and the tears ran down the father's cheeks.
A small hill, no mountain, higher than the level plain:
there their two bodies were given to the luckless flight.
And Daedalus moved his wings, and watched his son's,
and all the time kept to his own course.
Now Icarus delights in the strange journey,
and, fear forgotten, he flies more swiftly, with daring art.
A man catching fish, with quivering rod, saw them,
and the task he'd started dropped from his hand.
Now Samos was to the left (Naxos was far behind
and Paros, and Delos beloved by Phoebus the god)
Lebinthos lay to the right, and shady-wooded Calymne,
and Astypalaea ringed by rich fishing grounds,
when the boy, too rash, with youth's carelessness,
soared higher, and left his father far behind.
The knots give way, and the wax melts near the sun,
his flailing arms can't clutch at thin air.
Fearful, from heaven's heights he gazes at the deep:
terrified, darkness, born of fear, clouds his eyes.
The wax dissolves: he thrashes with naked arms,
and flutters there with nothing to support him.
He falls, and falling cries: 'Father, O father, I'm lost!'
the **salt–green** sea closes over his open **lips.**
But now the unhappy father, his father, calls, 'Icarus!
Where are you Icarus, where under the sky?
Calling 'Icarus', he saw the feathers on the waves.
Earth holds his bones: the waters take his name.

BOOK II PART II: YOU NEED GIFTS OF MIND

Minos could not **hold** back those mortal wings:
I'm setting out to check the winged god himself.
He who has recourse to Thracian magic, fails,
to what the foal yields, torn from its new-born brow,
Medea's herbs can't keep love alive,
nor Marsian dirges mingled with magic chants.
If incantations only could enslave love, Ulysses
would have been tied to Circe, Jason to the Colchian.
It's no use giving girls pale drugs:
drugs hurt the mind, have power to cause madness.
Away with such evils: to be loved be lovable:
something face and form alone won't give you.
Though you're Nireus loved by Homer of old,
or sweet Hylas ravished by the Naiades' crime,
to keep your love, and not to find her leave you,
add gifts of mind to grace of body.
A sweet form is fragile, what's added to its years
lessen it, and time itself eats it away.
Violets and open lilies do not flower forever,
and thorns are left stiffening on the blown rose.
And white hair will come to find you, lovely lad,
soon wrinkles will come, furrowing your skin.
Then nourish mind, which lasts, and adds to beauty:
it alone will stay till the funeral pyre.
Cultivate your thoughts with the noble arts,
more than a little, and learn two languages.
Ulysses wasn't handsome, but he was eloquent,
and still racked the sea-goddesses with love.
How often Calypso mourned his haste,
and denied the waves were fit for oars!

She asked him again and again about the fall of Troy:
He grew used to retelling it often, differently.
They walked the beach: there, lovely Calypso too
demanded the gory tale of King Rhesus's fate.
He, with a rod (a rod perhaps he already had)
illustrated what she asked in the thick sand.
'This' he said, 'is Troy' (drawing the walls in the sand):
'This your Simois: imagine this is our camp.
This is the field,' (he drew the field), 'that was dyed
with Dolon's blood, while he spied on Achilles's horses.
here were the tents of Thracian Rhesus:
here am I riding back the captured horses at night.'
And he was drawing more, when suddenly a wave
washed away Troy, and Rhesus, and his camp.
Then the goddess said 'Do you see what you place your trust in
for your voyage, waves that have destroyed such mighty names?'
So listen, whoever you are, fear to rely on treacherous beauty
or own to something more than just the flesh.

BOOK II PART III: GENTLE AND GOOD TEMPERED

Gentleness especially impresses minds favourably:
harshness creates hatred and fierce wars.
We hate the hawk that lives its life in battle,
and the wolf whose custom is to raid the timid flocks.
But the swallow, for its **gentleness**, is free from human snares,
and Chaonian doves have dovecotes to live in.
Away with disputes and the battle of bitter tongues:
sweet love must feed on gentle words.
Let married men and married women be checked by rebuffs,
and think in turn things always are against them:
that's proper for wives: quarrelling's the marriage dowry:
but a mistress should always hear the longed-for cooing.
No law orders you to come together in one bed:
in your rules it's love provides the entertainment.
Approach her with gentle flatteries and words to delight
her ear, so that your arrival makes her glad.
I don't come as a teacher of love for the rich:
he who can give has no need of my art:
He has genius who can say: 'Take this' when he pleases:
I submit: he delights more than my inventions
I'm the poor man's poet, who was poor when I loved:
when I could give no gifts, I gave them words.
The poor must love warily: the poor fear to speak amiss,
and suffer much that the rich would not.
I remember mussing my lady's hair in anger:
how many days that anger cost me!
I don't think I tore her dress, I didn't feel it: but she
said so, and my reward was to replace it.
But you, if you're wise, avoid your teacher's faults,
and fear the harm that came from my offence.

Make war with the Parthians, peace with a civilised friend,
and laughter, and **whatever engenders** love.

BOOK II PART IV: BE PATIENT AND COMPLY

If she's not charming or courteous enough, at your loving,
endure it and persist: she'll soon be kinder.
You can get a curved branch to bend on the tree by patience:
you'll break it, if you try out your full strength.
With patience you can cross the water: you'll not
conquer the river by sailing against the flow.
Patience tames tigers and Numidian lions:
the farmer in time bows the ox to the plough.
Who was fiercer than Arcadian Atalanta?
Wild as she was she still **surrender**ed to male kindness.
Often Milanion wept among the trees
at his plight and at the girl's harsh acts:
often at her orders his shoulders carried the nets,
often he pierced wild boars with his deadly spear:
and he felt the pain of Hylaeus's tense bow:
but that of another bow was still more familiar.
I don't order you to climb in Maenalian woods,
holding a weapon, or carrying nets on your back:
I don't order you to bare your chest to flying darts:
the tender commands of my arts are safe.
Yield to opposition: by yielding you'll end as victor:
Only play the part she commands you to.
Condemn what she condemns: what she approves, approve:
say what she says: deny what she denies.
She laughs, you laugh: **remember** to cry, if she cries:
she'll set the rules according to your expression.
If she plays, tossing the ivory dice in her hand,
throw them wrong, and concede on your bad throw:
If you play knucklebones, no prize if you win,
make out that often the ruinous low Dogs fell to you.

And if it's draughts, the draughtsmen mercenaries,
let your champion be swept away by your glass foe.
Yourself, hold your girl's sunshade outspread,
yourself, make a place for her in the crowd.
Quickly bring up a footstool to her elegant couch,
and slip the sandal on or off her sweet foot.
Often, even though you're shivering yourself,
her hand must be warmed at your neglected breast.
Don't think it shameful (though it's shameful, you'll like it),
to hold the mirror for her in your noble hands.
When his stepmother, Juno, was tired of sending him monsters,
Hercules, it's said, who reached the heavens he'd shouldered,
held a basket, among the Lydian girls, and spun raw wool.
The hero of Tiryns complied with his girl's orders:
go now, and endure the misgivings he endured.
Ordered to appear in town, make sure you arrive
before time, and don't leave unless it's late.
She tells you to be elsewhere: drop **everything**, run,
don't let the crowd in the way stop you trying.
She's returning home from another party at night:
when she calls for her slave you come too.
She's in the country, says: 'come': Love hates a laggard:
if you've no wheels, travel the road on foot.
Don't let bad weather, or parching Dog-days, stall you,
or the roads whitened by falling snow.

BOOK II PART V: DON'T BE FAINT-HEARTED

L ove is a kind of warfare. Slackers, dismiss!
There are no cowards guarding this standard.
Night and winter, long roads and cruel sorrows,
and every kind of labour are found on love's campaigns.
You'll often endure rain pouring from heavenly clouds,
and frozen, **lie there on** the naked earth.
They say that Phoebus grazed Admetus's cattle,
and found shelter in a humble hut.
Who can't suit what suited Phoebus? Lose your pride,
you who'd have love's sorrows tamed.
If you're denied a safe and level road,
and the door barred with a bolt against you,
then drop down head-first through **the open roof**:
a high window too offers a secret way.
She'll be glad, knowing the **chase** itself is risky for you:
that will be sure proof to **the** lady of your love.
You might often have been parted from your girl, Leander:
you swam across so she could know your **heart**.

BOOK II PART VI: WIN OVER THE SERVANTS

Nor is it shameful to you to cultivate her maids,
according to their grades, and the serving men.
Greet them by their names (it costs you nothing)
clasp humble hands with yours, in your ambition.
And even offer the servant, who asks, a little something
on Fortune's Day (it's little enough to pay):
and the maid, on that day when the hand **of** punishment fell
on the Gauls, they deluded by maids in mistress's clothes.
Trust me, make the people yours: especially the gatekeeper,
and whoever lies in front of her bedroom doors.

BOOK II PART VII: GIVE HER LITTLE TASTEFUL GIFTS

I don't tell you to give your mistress expensive gifts:
give little but of that little, skilfully, give what's fitting.
When the field is full of riches, when the branches bend
with the weight, let the boy bring a gift in a rustic basket.
You can say it was sent from **your** country villa,
even though it was bought on the Via Sacra.
Send grapes, or those nuts Amaryllis loved,
chestnuts, but she doesn't love them now.
Why even thrushes are fine, and the gift of a dove,
to witness your remembrance of your mistress.
Shameful to send them hoping for the death of some childless
old man. Ah, perish those who make giving a crime!
Do I also teach that you send tender verses?
Ah me, poems are not honoured much.
Songs are praised, but it's gifts they really want:
barbarians themselves are pleasing, so long as they're rich.
Truly now it is the Age of Gold: the greatest honours
come with gold: love's won by gold.
Even if you came, Homer, with the Muses as companions,
if you brought nothing with you, Homer, you'd be out.
Still there are cultured girls, the rarest set:
and another set who aren't, but would like to be.
Praise either in song: and they'll commend
the **reader** whatever his voice's sweetness:
So sing your midnight song to one and the other,
perhaps it will figure as a trifling gift.

BOOK II PART VIII: FAVOUR HER AND COMPLIMENT HER

Then what you're about to do, and think is useful,
always get your lover to ask you to do it.
You promised liberty to one of your slaves:
still let him seek the fact of it from your girl:
if you stay a punishment, forgo the use of cruel chains,
let her be thankful to you, for what you did:
the advantage is yours: the title 'giver' is your lover's:
you lose nothing, she plays the mistress's part.
But whoever you are, who want to keep your girl,
she must think that you're inspired by her beauty.
If she's dressed in Tyrian robes, praise Tyrian:
if she's in Coan silk, consider Coan fitting.
She's in gold-thread? She's more precious than gold:
She wears wool, approve the wool she's wearing.
She leaves off her tunic, cry: 'You set me on fire',
but request her anxiously to beware of chills.
She's parted her hair: praise the parting:
she waves her hair: be pleased with the waves.
Admire her limbs as she dances, her voice when she sings,
and when it finishes, grieve that it's finished in words.
It's fine if you tell her what delights, **and** what gives joy
about her lovemaking, her skill in bed.
Though she's more violent than fierce Medusa,
she'll be 'kind and gentle' to her lover.
But make sure of this: don't let **your** expression
give your speech the lie, lest you seem a deceiver with words.
Art works when it's hidden: discovery brings shame,
and time destroys faith in everything of merit.

BOOK II PART IX: COMFORT HER IN SICKNESS

Often in autumn, when the season's **loveliest**,
and the ripe grape's dyed with purple juice,
when now we're frozen solid, now drenched with heat,
the body's listless in the changing air.
Your girl's well in fact: but if she's lying sick,
feels ill because of the unhealthy weather,
then let love and devotion be obvious to your girl,
then sow what you'll reap later with full sickle.
Don't be put off by the fretfulness of the patient,
let yours be the hand that does what she allows.
And be seen weeping, and don't shrink from kisses,
let her parched mouth drink from your tears.
Pray a lot, but all aloud: and, as often as she lets you,
tell her happy dreams that you remembered.
And let the old woman come who cleanses room and bed,
bringing sulphur and eggs in her trembling hands.
The signs of a welcome devotion are in all this:
by these means into wills many have made their way.
But don't let dislike for your attentions rise from illness,
only be charming, in your earnestness:
don't prohibit food, or hand her cups of bitter stuff:
let your **rival** mix all that for her.

BOOK II PART X: LET HER MISS YOU: BUT NOT FOR LONG

Ｂut the winds that filled your sails and blew offshore,
are no use when you're in the open sea.
While young love's wandering, it gathers strength by use:
if you nourish it well, it will be strong in time.
The bull you fear's the calf you used to stroke:
the tree you lie beneath was a sapling:
the river's tiny when born, but **gather**s riches in its flow,
and collects the many waters that come to it.
Make her accustomed to you: nothing's greater than habit:
while you're captivating her, avoid no boredom.
Let her always be seeing you: always giving you ear:
show your face, at night and in the day.
When you've more confidence that you'll be missed,
when your absence far away will cause her worry,
give her a rest: the fields when rested repay the loan,
and parched earth drinks the heavenly rain.
Phyllis burnt less for Demophoon in his presence:
she blazed more fiercely when he sailed away.
Penelope was tormented by the loss of cunning Ulysses:
you, Laodamia, by absent Protesilaus.
But brief delays are best: fondness fades with time,
love vanishes with **absence**, and new love appears.
When Menelaus left, Helen did not lie alone,
Paris, the guest, at night, was taken to her warm breast.
What craziness was that, Menelaus? You left
wife and guest alone under the same roof.
Madman, would you trust timid doves to a hawk?
Would you trust the full fold to a mountain wolf?
Helen did not sin: her lover committed none:
what you, what anyone would do, he did.

You forced adultery by giving time and place:
What did the girl employ but your counsel?
What should she do? Her man away, a **cultivate**d guest,
and she afraid to sleep alone in an empty bed.
Let Atrides appear: I acquit Helen of crime:
she took advantage of her husband's courtesy.

BOOK II PART XI: HAVE OTHER FRIENDS: BUT BE CAREFUL

But the red-haired boar is not so fierce in mid-anger.
when he turns and threatens the rabid pack,
or the lioness giving suck to un-weaned cubs,
or the tiny viper crushed by a careless foot,
as a woman when a rival's caught in her lover's bed:
she blazes, her face the colour of her heart.
She storms with fire and flame, all restraint forgot,
as if struck, as they say, by the horns of the Boeotian god.
Wronged by her husband, her marriage violated,
savage Medea avenged herself through her children.
Another fatal mother was that swallow, you see there:
look, her breast carries the stain of blood.
Well-founded and firm loves have been dissolved so:
these are crimes to make cautious men afraid.
Not that my censure condemns you to only one girl:
the gods forbid! A wife could hardly expect that.
Indulge, but secretly veil your sins, with restraint:
it's no glory to you to be seeking out wrongdoing.
Don't give gifts another girl could spot,
or have set times for your assignations.
And lest a girl catch you out in **your** favourite haunts
don't meet all of them in one place.
And always look closely at your wax tablets, whenever you write:
lest much more is read there than you sent.
Wounded, Venus takes up just arms, and hurls her dart,
and makes you lament, as she is lamenting.
While Agamemnon was satisfied with one woman, Clytemnestra
was chaste: evil was done through the man's fault.
She had heard how Chryses, with sacred head-bands,
and laurel in his hand, failed to win back his daughter:

she had heard of your **sorrow**s, captive Briseis,
and how scandalous delays had prolonged the war.
She heard all this: She saw Cassandra for herself:
the victor the shameful prize of his own prize.
Then she took Thyestes to her heart and bed,
and wrongfully avenged the Atrides's crime.
Even if the acts, you've well hidden, become known,
though they're known, still always deny them.
Don't be subdued, or more fond than usual:
those are the signs of many guilty thoughts.
But don't forgo sex: all peace is in that one thing.
The act it is that disproves a prior union.

BOOK II PART XII: APHRODISIACS?

There are those who prescribe eating a dish of savory,
a noxious herb, my judgement is it's poisonous:
or mix pepper with the seeds of stinging nettles,
or crush yellow camomile in well-aged wine:
But the goddess who holds high Eryx, beneath the shaded hill,
doesn't force you to suffer like this for her delights.
White onions brought from Megara, Alcathous's city,
and rocket, herba salax, the kind that comes from **garden**s,
eat **those**, and eggs, eat honey from Hymettus,
and **seeds** from the cones of sharp-needled pines.

BOOK II PART XIII: STIR HER JEALOUSY

Wise Erato, why turn to magic arts?
  My chariot's scraping the inside post.
You who just hid your crimes on my advice,
change course, and on my advice reveal your secrets.
I'm not guilty of fickleness: the curved prow
is not always blown onwards by the same wind.
Now we run to a Thracian northerly, an easterly now,
sometimes a west wind fills our sails, sometimes a south.
Look how the charioteer now slacks the reins,
then skilfully restrains the galloping team.
There are those who don't like being served with shy kindness:
while love fades if there's no rival around.
Generally heads **are swollen with** success,
it's not easy to be content with the good times.
As a fire with little power, gradually consumed,
hides itself, ashes whitening on its surface,
but the doused flames will flare with a pinch of sulphur,
and the **brightness**, that was there before, returns:
so when hearts are numbed by slack dullness and security,
love is aroused by some sharp stimulus.
Make her fearful for you: warm her tepid mind:
let her grow pale at evidence of your guilt:
O four times happy, times impossible to count,
is he for whom his wounded girl grieves.
That, when his sins reach her unwilling ears, she's lost,
and voice and colour flee the unhappy girl.
Let me be him, whose hair the angry woman tears:
let me be him, whose tender cheeks nails seek,
him whom she sees with tears, turns on him tortured eyes,
whom though she can't live without, she wishes she could.

If you ask how long you should let her lament her hurt,
keep it brief, lest a long delay kindles anger's force:
Throw your arms straightaway around her snow-white neck,
and let the weeping girl fall on your chest.
Kiss her who weeps, make sweet love to her who weeps,
there'll be peace: this is the one way anger's dissolved.
When she's truly raging, when she seems fixed on war,
then sue for peace in bed, she'll be gentle.
There Harmony dwells with grounded arms:
there, trust me, is the place where grace is born.
Doves that once fought, now bill and coo,
whose murmur is of caressing words.
At first all things were confused mass without form,
heaven and earth and sea were created one:
soon sky was set above land, earth circled by water,
and random chaos split into its parts:
Forests **allow**ed the creatures a home: air the birds:
fish took shelter in the running streams.
Then the human race wandered the empty wilds,
a thing of naked strength and brutish body:
woods were its home, grass its food, leaves its bed:
and for a long time no man knew another.
They say sweet delights softened savage spirits:
when man and woman rested in one place:
they had no teacher to show them what to do:
Venus did her work without sweet art.
Birds have mates to love: in the midst of waters
a fish will find another to share her joy:
hind follows stag, snake will bind with snake,
bitch clings entwined with some adulterous dog:
ewes delight in being covered: bulls delight in heifers, too,
the snub-nosed she-goat supports her rank mate:
Mares driven to frenzy follow their stallion,
through distant places beyond the branching river.
So act, and offer strong medicine to **your** angry one:

only this will bring peace to her un**happiness**:
this medicine beats Machaon's drugs:
this will reinstate you when you've sinned.

BOOK II PART XIV: BE WISE AND SUFFER

While I was writing this, Apollo suddenly appeared
plucking the strings of his lyre with his thumb.
Laurel was in his hand, laurel wreathing his hair:
he appears to poets looking like that.
'Professor of Wanton Love,' he said to me,
'go lead your disciples to my temple,
it's where the famous words, celebrated throughout the world,
command everyone to "Know Yourself".
He alone will be wise, who's well-known to himself,
and carries out each work that suits his powers.
Whom nature's given beauty, let it **be seen** by her:
whose skin is lustrous, lie there often with bare shoulders:
who delights by talking, avoid taciturn silence:
who sings with art, then sing: who drinks with art, then drink.
but the eloquent should never declaim mid-speech
nor the crazy poet ever read his poems!'
So Phoebus warned: take note of Phoebus's warning:
truth's surely on the sacred lips of that god.
To bring us back to earth: who loves wisely wins,
and by my skill will bring off what he seeks.
It's not often the furrow repays the loan with interest,
not often the winds aid the boat in trouble:
What delights a lover is little, what pains him more:
many sufferings declare themselves to his heart.
As many as hares on Athos, the bees that graze on Hybla,
as many as the olives the grey-green branches **carry**,
or the **sea-shells** on the shore, are the pains of love:
the thorns we suffer from are drenched **in** gall.
They'll say she's gone out: very likely she's to be seen inside:
think that she has gone out, and your vision lied.

The door will be shut **the night** she promised you:
endure it, lay your body on the dusty ground.
And perhaps the lying maid with scornful face,
will say: 'Why's he hanging round our door?'
Still, a suppliant, coax the doorposts, and your harsh mistress,
and hang the roses, from your head, outside.
Come if she wishes: when she shuns you, go:
it's unbecoming to a noble man to bore her.
Why let your lover say: 'There's no escaping him'?
Her feelings won't always be against you.
Don't think it a disgrace to suffer curses or blows
from the girl, or plant kisses on her tender feet.

BOOK II PART XV: RESPECT HER FREEDOM

Why waste time on trifles? Greater themes arise:
I sing great things: pay attention, people.
We labour hard, but virtue's nothing if not hard:
hard labour's what my art demands.
Be patient with your rival, victory rests with you:
you'll be victor on Great Jupiter's hill.
Believe me, it's no man says this, but Chaonia's sacred oaks:
my art contains nothing more profound than this.
If she flirts, endure it: if she writes, don't touch the wax:
let her come from where she wishes: and go where she pleases, too.
This husbands allow their lawfully married wives,
when you come, gentle sleep, to play your part, as well.
I'm not perfect in this art, I confess:
What can I do? I'm less than my own instructions.
What, shall I let some man signal openly to my girl,
and bear it, and not show anger if I wish?
I remember her husband kissed her: I grieved
at the kiss he gave: my love's full of barbarities.
Not a few times this fault has hurt me: he's wiser
who's reconciled to other mens' coming.
But it was better to know nothing: let intrigues
be hidden, lest her shameless mouth revealed untruths.
How much better, O young men, to avoid surprising them:
let girls sin, and think, while sinning, that they've fooled you.
Love grows with being caught: who are twinned by fortune
persist to the end in the cause that ruined them.
The story's well known through all the heavens,
of Mars and Venus caught by Vulcan's craft.
Mars stirred by mad desire for Venus
was turned from grim warrior to lover.
And Venus was not coy or resistant to Mar's pleas

(for there's no more loving goddess than her).
Ah how often the wanton laughed at her husband's limp,
they say, or his hands hardened by his fiery art.
She'd openly imitate Vulcan then, to Mars: it became her:
great beauty was mingled there with charm.
But they used to hide their adultery at first.
It was a sin, filled with the blush of shame.
The Sun's tale (who can evade the Sun?)
made known to Vulcan what his spouse had done.
What a poor example, Sun, you set! Seek a gift from her,
and you, if you're quiet, can have what she can give.
Vulcan set a hidden net, over and round the bed:
it's a piece of work that deceives the eye.
Pretends he's off to Lemnos: the lovers come
to their assignation: and both lie naked in the net.
He calls the gods: the captives are displayed:
Venus they think can scarcely restrain her tears.
They can't hide their faces, are **even** unable
to cover their sexes with their hands.
Then someone laughed and said: 'Let me have the chains,
Mars, **if** they're an embarrassment to you!'
Their captive bodies are, with difficulty, freed, at your plea,
Neptune: Venus runs to Paphos: Mars heads for Thrace.
This you achieved, Vulcan: what they hid before,
now all shame is gone, they indulge in freely:
Now maddened you often confess the thing was foolish,
and suffer regret for your cunning.
It's forbidden you: Venus once tricked forbids
traps to be set, like the one that she endured.
Lay out no snares for rivals: don't intercept
those secret hand-written messages.
Let husbands trap them, if they think they indeed need trapping,
husbands to whom the ceremony of fire and water gives the right.
Look, I swear again: there's nothing here except what's played
within the law: no virtuous woman's caught up in my jests.

BOOK II PART XVI: KEEP IT SECRET

Who'd dare reveal to the impious the secret rites of Ceres,
or uncover the high mysteries of Samothrace?
There's little virtue in keeping silent:
but speaking of what's kept secret's a heinous crime.
O it's good if that babbler Tantalus, clutching at fruit in vain,
thirsts in the very middle of the waters!
Venus, above all, orders you to be silent about her rites:
I warn **you**, let no idle chatterers come near her.
Though the mysteries of Venus are not buried in a box,
nor echo in the wide air to the clash of cymbals,
but are busily enjoyed so, by us all,
they still wish to be concealed among us.
Venus, herself, when she takes off her clothes,
covers her sex with the half-turned palm of her left hand.
Beasts couple indiscriminately in full view: from this sight
girls of course turn aside their faces, too.
Bedrooms and locked doors suit our intrigues,
and shameful things are hidden under the sheets:
and if not darkness, we seek some veiling shadow,
and something less exposed than the light of day.
Even back then, when roofs kept out neither rain nor sun,
and the oak-tree provided food and shelter,
pleasure was had in woods and caves, not under the heavens:
such care the native peoples had for their modesty.
but now we advertise our nocturnal acts,
and nothing's bought if it can't be boasted of!
No doubt you'll look out every girl, whatever,
to say to whom you please: 'She too was mine,'
and there'll be no lack of those you can point out,
so for each that's mentioned there's a shameful tale?

Little to cry at: some invent, what they'd deny if true,
and claim there isn't one they haven't slept with.
If not their bodies, they touch what they can, their names,
and the reputation's gone, though the body's chaste.
Odious watchman, go close the girl's door, now,
too late, locked with a hundred heavy bars!
What's safe, when adulterers give out her name,
and want what **never** happened to be **believed**?
I'm wary even of professing to genuine passions,
and, trust me, my secret affairs are wholly hidden.

BOOK II PART XVII: DON'T MENTION HER FAULTS

Above all beware of reproaching girls for their faults,
it's useful to ignore so many things.
Andromeda's dark complexion was not criticised
by Perseus, who was borne aloft by wings on his feet.
Andromache by all was rightly thought too tall:
Hector was the only one who spoke of her as small.
Grow accustomed to what's called bad, you'll call it good:
Time heals much: new love feels everything.
While a new-grafted twig's growing in the green bark,
struck by the lightest breeze, it may fall:
Later, hardened by time, it resists the winds,
and the strong tree will bear adopted wealth.
Time itself erases all faults from the flesh,
and what was a flaw, ceases to make you pause.
A new ox-hide makes nostrils recoil:
tamed by familiarity, the odour fades.
An evil may be sweetened by its name: let her be 'dark'
whose pigment's blacker than Illyrian pitch:
if she squints, she's like Venus: if she's grey, Minerva:
let her be 'slender', who's truly emaciated:
call her 'trim', who's tiny, 'full-bodied' if she's gross,
and hide the fault behind the nearest virtue.

BOOK II PART XVIII: DON'T ASK ABOUT HER AGE

Don't ask how old she is, or who was Consul when
she was born, that's strictly the Censor's duty:
Especially if she's past bloom, and the good times gone,
and now she plucks the odd grey hair.
There's value, O youth, in this or a greater age:
this will bear seed, this is a field to sow.
Besides, they've more knowledge of the thing,
and have that practice that alone makes the artist:
With elegance they repair the marks of time,
and take good care that they don't appear old.
As you wish, they'll perform in **a thousand** positions:
no painting's ever contrived to show more ways.
They don't have to be aroused to pleasure:
man and woman equally deliver what delights.
I hate sex that doesn't provide release for both:
that's why the touch of boys is less desirable.
I hate a girl who gives because she has to,
and, arid herself, thinks only of her spinning.
Pleasure's no joy to me that's given out of duty:
let no girl be dutiful to me.
I like to hear a voice confessing to her rapture,
which begs me to hold back, and keep on going.
I gaze at the dazed **eyes** of my frantic mistress:
she's exhausted, and won't let herself be touched for ages.
Nature doesn't give those joys to raw youths,
that often come so easily beyond thirty-five.
The hasty drink the new and unfermented: pour a vintage wine
for me, matured in the cask, from an ancient consulship.
Not till it's grown can the plane tree bear the sun,
and naked feet destroy a new-laid lawn.

I suppose you'd prefer Hermione to Helen,
and was Medusa any better than her mother?
Then, he who wants to come to his love late,
earns a valuable prize, if he'll only **wait.**

BOOK II PART XIX: DON'T RUSH

See, the knowing bed receives two lovers:
halt, Muse, at the closed doors of the room.
Flowing words will be said, by themselves, without you:
and that left hand won't lie idle on the bed.
Fingers will find what will arouse those parts,
where love's dart is dipped in secrecy.
Hector did it once with vigour, for Andromache,
and wasn't only useful in the wars.
And great Achilles did it for his captive maid,
when he lay in his sweet bed, weary from the fight.
You let yourself be touched by hands, Briseis,
that were still dyed with Trojan blood.
And was that what overjoyed you, lascivious girl,
those conquering fingers approaching your body?
Trust me, love's pleasure's not to be hurried,
but to be felt enticingly with lingering delays.
When you've reached the place, where a girl loves to be touched,
don't let modesty prevent you touching her.
You'll see her eyes flickering with tremulous brightness,
as sunlight often flashes from running water.
Moans and loving murmurs will arise,
and sweet sighs, and playful and fitting words.
But don't desert your mistress by cramming on more sail,
or let her overtake you in your race:
hasten to the goal together: that's the fullness of pleasure,
when man and woman lie there equally spent.
This is the pace you should indulge in, when you're given
time for leisure, and fear does not urge on the secret **work.**
When delay's not safe, lean usefully on the oar,
and plunge your spur into the galloping horse.

While strength and years allow, sustain the work:
bent age **come**s soon enough on silent feet.
Plough the earth with the blade, the sea with oars,
take a cruel weapon in your warring hands,
or spend your body, and strength, and time, on girls:
this is warlike service too, this **to**o earns plenty.

BOOK II PART XX: THE TASK'S COMPLETE ... BUT NOW ...

The end of the work's at hand: grateful youth grant me the palm,
and set the wreathe of myrtle on my perfumed hair.
As Podalirius with his art of medicine, among the Greeks,
was great, Achilles with his right hand, Nestor his wisdom,
Calchas great as a prophet, Ajax in arms,
Automedon as a charioteer, so am I in love.
Celebrate me as a poet, men, speak my praises,
let my name be sung throughout the world.
I've given you weapons: Vulcan gave Achilles his:
excel with **the** gifts you're given, as he excelled.
But whoever overcomes an Amazon with my sword,
write on the spoils 'Ovid was my master.'
Behold, you **tender** girls ask for rules for yourselves:
well yours then will be the next task for my **pen**!

BOOK III

BOOK III PART I: IT'S TIME TO TEACH YOU GIRLS

I've given the Greeks arms, against Amazons: arms remain,
to give to you Penthesilea, and your Amazon troop.
Go equal to the fight: let them win, those who are favoured
by Venus, and her Boy, who flies through all the world.
It's not fair for armed men to battle with naked girls:
that would be shameful, men, even if you win.
Someone will say: 'Why add venom to the snake,
and betray the sheepfold to the rabid she-wolf?'
Beware of loading the crime of **the many** onto the few:
let the merits of each separate girl be seen.
Though Menelaus has Helen, and Agamemnon
has Clytemnestra, her sister, to charge with crime,
though Amphiarus, and his horses too, came living to the Styx,
through the wickedness of Eriphyle,
Penelope was faithful to her husband for all ten years
of his waging war, and his ten years wandering.
Think of Protesilaus, and Laodameia who they say
followed her marriage partner, died before her time.
Alcestis, his wife, redeemed Admetus's life with her own:
the wife, for the man, was borne to the husband's funeral.
'Capaneus, receive me! Let us mingle our ashes,'
Evadne cried, and leapt into the flames.
Virtue herself is named and worshipped as a woman too:
it's no wonder that she delights her followers.
Yet their aims are not required for my art,
smaller sails are suited to my boat,
Only playful passions will be learnt from me:
I'll teach girls the ways of being loved.
Women don't brandish flames or cruel bows:
I rarely see men harmed by their weapons.

Men often cheat: it's seldom tender girls,
and, if you check, they're rarely accused of fraud.
Falsely, Jason left Medea, already a mother:
he took another bride to himself.
As far as you knew, Theseus, the sea birds fed on Ariadne,
left all by herself on an unknown island!
Ask why one road's called Nine-Times and hear
how the woods, weeping, shed their leaves for Phyllis.
Though he might be famed for piety, Aeneas, your guest,
supplied the sword, Dido, and the reason for your death.
What destroyed you all, I ask? Not knowing how to love:
your art was lacking: love lasts long through art.
You still might lack it now: but, before my eyes,
stood Venus herself, and ordered me to teach you.
She said to me, then: 'What have the poor girls done,
an unarmed crowd betrayed to well-armed men?
Two books of their tricks have been composed:
let this lot too be instructed by your **warnings**.
Stesichorus who spoke against Helen's un-chastity,
soon sang her praises in a happier key.
If I know you well (don't harm the cultured girls now!)
this favour will always be asked of you while you live.'
She spoke, and she gave me a leaf, and a few myrtle
berries (since her hair was crowned with myrtle):
I felt received power too: purer air
glowed, and a whole weight lifted from my spirit.
While wit works, seek your orders here girls,
those that modesty, principles and your rules allow.
Be mindful first that old age will come to you:
so don't be timid and waste any of your time.
Have fun while it's allowed, while your years are in their prime:
the years go by like flowing waters:
The wave that's past can't be recalled again,
the hour that's past never can return.
Life's to be used: life slips by on swift feet,

what was good at first, nothing as good will follow.
Those stalks that wither I saw as violets:
from that thorn-bush to me a dear garland was given.
There'll be a time when you, who now shut out your lover,
will lie alone, and aged, in the cold of night,
nor find your entrance damaged by some nocturnal quarrel,
nor your threshold sprinkled with roses at dawn.
How quickly (ah me!) the sagging flesh wrinkles,
and the colour, there, is lost from the bright cheek.
And hairs that you'll swear were grey **from your girlhood**
will spring up all over your head overnight.
Snakes shed their old age with their fragile skin,
antlers that are cast make the stag seem young:
un-aided our beauties flee: pluck the flower,
which, if not plucked, will of itself, shamefully, fall.
Add that the time of youth is shortened by childbirth:
the field's exhausted by continual harvest.
Endymion causes you no blushes, on Latmos, Moon,
nor is Cephalus the rosy goddess of Dawn's shameful prize.
Though Adonis was given to Venus, whom she mourns to this day,
where did she get Aeneas, and Harmonia, from?
O mortal girls go to the goddesses **for** your **example**s,
and don't deny your delights to loving men.
Even if you're deceived, what do you lose? It's all intact:
though a thousand use it, nothing's destroyed that way.
Iron crumbles, stone's worn away with use:
that part's sufficient, and escapes all fear of harm.
Who objects to taking light from a light nearby?
Who hoards the vast waters of the hollow deep?
So why should any woman say: 'Not now'? Tell me,
why waste the water if you're not going to use it?
Nor does my voice say sell it, just don't **be afraid**
of casual loss: your gifts are freed from loss.

BOOK III PART II: CARE WITH HOW YOU LOOK

But I'm blown about by greater gusts of wind,
while we're in harbour, may you ride the gentle breeze.
I'll start with how you look: good wine comes from vines
that are looked after, tall crops stand in cultivated soil.
Beauty's a gift of the gods: how many can boast it?
The larger number among you lack such gifts.
Taking pains brings beauty: beauty neglected dies,
even though it's like that of Venus, the Idalian goddess.
If girls of old didn't cultivate their bodies in that way,
well they had no cultivated men in those days:
if Andromache was dressed in healthy clothes,
what wonder? Her husband was a rough soldier?
Do you suppose Ajax's wife would come to him all smart,
when his outer layer was seven hides of an ox?
There was crude simplicity before: now Rome is golden,
and owns the vast wealth of the conquered world.
Look what the Capitol is now, and what it was:
you'd say it belonged to a different Jove.
The Senate-House, now worthy of such debates,
was made of wattle when Tatius held the kingship.
Where the Palatine now gleams with Apollo and our leaders,
what was that but pasture for ploughmen's oxen?
Others may delight in ancient times: I congratulate myself
on having been born just now: this age suits my nature.
Not because **stubborn** gold's mined now from the earth,
or choice shells come to us from farthest shores:
nor because mountains shrink as marble's quarried,
or because blue waters retreat from the piers:
but because civilisation's here, and no crudity remains,
in our age, that survives from our ancient ancestors.

You too shouldn't weight your ears with costly stones,
that dusky India gathers in its green waters,
nor show yourself in stiff clothes sewn with gold,
wealth which you court us with, often makes us flee.

BOOK III PART III: TASTE AND ELEGANCE IN HAIR AND DRESS

We're captivated by elegance: don't ignore your hair:
beauty's granted or denied by a hand's touch.
There isn't only one style: choose what suits each one,
and consult your mirror in advance.
An oval-shaped head suggests a plain parting:
that's how Laodamia arranged her hair.
A round face asks for a small knot on the top,
leaving the forehead free, showing the ears.
One girl should throw her hair over both shoulders:
like Phoebus when he takes up the lyre to sing.
Another tied up behind, in Diana's usual style,
when, skirts tucked up, she seeks the frightened quarry.
Blown tresses suit this girl, loosely scattered:
that one's encircled by tight-bound hair.
This one delights in being adorned by tortoiseshell from Cyllene:
that one presents a likeness to **the** curves of a wave.
But you'll no more number the acorns on oak branches,
or bees on Hybla, wild beasts on Alpine mountains,
than I can possibly count so many fashions:
every new day adds another new style.
And tangled hair suits many girls: often you'd think
it's been hanging loose since yesterday: it's just combed.
Art imitates chance: when Hercules, in captured Oechalia,
saw Iole like that, he said: 'I love that girl.'
So you Bacchus, lifted forsaken Ariadne,
into your chariot, while the Satyrs gave their cries.
O how kind nature is to your beauty,
how many ways you have to repair the damage!
We're sadly exposed, and our hair, snatched at by time,
falls like the leaves stripped by the north wind.

A woman dyes the grey with German herbs,
and seeks a better colour by their art:
a woman shows herself in dense bought curls,
instead of her own, pays cash for another's.
No blushes shown: you can see them coming, openly,
before the eyes of Hercules and the Virgin Muses Choir.
What to say about dress? Don't ask for brocade,
or wools dyed purple with Tyrian murex.
With so many cheaper colours having appeared,
it's crazy to bear your fortune on your back!
See, the **sky's colour,** when the sky's without a cloud,
no warm south-westerly threatening heavy rain.
See, what to you, you'll say, looks similar to that fleece,
on which Phrixus and Helle once escaped fierce Ino:
this resembles the waves, and also takes its name from the waves:
I might have thought the sea-nymphs clothed with this veil.
That's like saffron-flowers: dressed in saffron robes,
the dew-wet goddess yokes her shining horses:
this, Paphian myrtle: this, purple amethyst,
dawn roses, and the Thracian crane's grey.
Your chestnuts are not lacking, Amaryllis, and almonds:
and wax gives its name to various wools.
As many as the flowers the new world, in warm spring, bears
when vine-buds wake, and dark winter vanishes,
as many or more dyes the wool drinks: choose, **decisive**ly:
since all are not suitable for everyone.
dark-grey suits snow-white skin: dark-grey suited Briseis:
when she was carried off, then she also wore dark-grey.
White suits the dark: you looked pleasing, Andromeda, in white:
so dressed, the island of Seriphos was ruled by you.

BOOK III PART IV: MAKE-UP, BUT IN PRIVATE

How near I was to warning you, no rankness of the wild goat
under your armpits, no legs bristling with harsh hair!
But I'm not teaching girls from the Caucasian hills,
or those who drink your waters, Mysian Caicus.
So why remind you not to let your teeth get blackened,
by being lazy, and to wash your face each morning in water?
You know how to acquire whiteness with a layer of powder:
she who doesn't blush by blood, indeed, blushes by art.
You make good the naked edges of your eyebrows,
and hide your natural cheeks with little patches.
It's no shame to highlight your eyes with thinned **as**hes,
or saffron grown by your banks, bright Cydnus.
It's I who spoke of facial treatments for your beauty,
a little book, but one whose labour took great care.
There too you can find protection against faded looks:
my art's no idle thing in your behalf.
Still, don't let your lover find cosmetic bottles
on your dressing table: art delights in its hidden face.
Who's not offended by cream smeared all over your face,
when it runs in fallen drops to your warm breast?
Don't those ointments smell? Even if they are sent from Athens,
they're oils extracted from the unwashed fleece of a sheep.
Don't apply preparations of deer marrow openly,
and I don't approve of openly cleaning your **teeth**:
it makes for beauty, but it's not beautiful to watch:
many things that please when done, are ugly in the doing:
What now carries the signature of busy Myron
was once dumb mass, hard stone:
to make a ring, first crush the golden ore:
the dress you wear, was greasy wool:

That was rough marble, now it forms a famous statue,
naked Venus squeezing water from her wet hair.
We'll think you too are sleeping while you do your face:
fit to be seen after the final touches.
Why should I know the source of the brightness in your looks?
Close your bedroom door! Why betray unfinished work?
There are many things it's right men shouldn't know:
most things offend if you don't keep them secret.
The golden figures shining from the ornate theatre,
examine them, you'll despise them: gilding hiding wood:
but the crowd's not allowed to approach them till they're done,
and till your beauty's ready banish men.
But I don't **forbid** your hair being freely combed,
so that it falls, loosely spread, across your shoulders.
Beware especially lest you're irritable then,
or are always loosening your failed hairstyle again.
Leave your maid alone: I hate those who scratch her face
with their nails, or prick the arm they've snatched at with a pin.
She'll curse her mistress's head at every touch,
as she weeps, bleeding, on the hateful tresses.
If you're hair's appalling, set a guard at your threshold,
or always have it done at Bona Dea's fertile temple.
I was once suddenly announced arriving at some girl's:
in her confusion she put her hair on wrong way round.
May such cause of cruel shame come to my enemies,
and that disgrace be reserved for Parthian girls.
Hornless cows are ugly, fields are ugly without grass,
and bushes without leaves, and a head without its hair.

BOOK III PART V: CONCEAL YOUR DEFECTS

I've not come to teach Semele or Leda, or Sidon's Europa,
carried through the waves by that deceptive bull,
or Helen, whom Menelaus, being no fool, reclaimed,
and you, Paris, her Trojan captor, also no fool, withheld.
The crowd come to be taught, girls pretty and plain:
and always the greater part are not-so-good.
The beautiful ones don't seek art and instruction:
they have their dowry, beauty potent without art:
the sailor rests secure when the sea's calm:
when it's swollen, he uses every aid.
Still, faultless forms are rare: conceal your faults,
and hide your body's defects as best you may.
If you're short sit down, lest, standing, you seem to sit:
and commit **your smallness** to your couch:
there also, so your measure can't be taken,
let a shawl drop over your feet to hide them.
If you're very slender, wear a full dress, and walk about
in clothes that hang loosely from your shoulders.
A pale girl scatters bright stripes across her body,
the darker then have recourse to linen from Alexandria.
Let an ugly foot be hidden in snow-white leather:
and don't loose the bands from skinny legs.
Thin padding suits those with high shoulder blades:
a good brassiere goes with a meagre chest.
Those with thick fingers **and** bitten nails,
make sparing use of gestures whenever you speak.
Those with strong breath don't talk when you're fasting.
and always keep your mouth a distance from your lover.

BOOK III PART VI: BE MODEST IN LAUGHTER AND MOVEMENT

If you're teeth are blackened, large, or not in line
from birth, laughing would be a fatal error.
Who'd believe it? Girls must even learn to laugh,
they **seek** to acquire beauty also in this way.
Laugh modestly, a small dimple either side,
the teeth mostly concealed by the lips.
Don't strain your lungs with continual laughter,
but let something soft and feminine ring out.
One girl will distort her face perversely by guffawing:
another shakes with laughter, you'd think she's crying.
That one laughs stridently in a hateful manner,
like a mangy ass braying at the shameful mill.
Where does art not penetrate? They're taught to cry,
with propriety, they weep when and how they wish.
Why! Aren't true words cheated by the voice,
and tongues forced to make lisping sounds to order?
Charm's in a defect: they try to speak badly:
they're taught, when they can speak, to speak less.
Weigh all this with care, since it's for you:
learn to carry yourself in a feminine way.
And not the least part of charm is in walking:
it attracts men you don't know, or sends them running.
One moves her hips with art, catches the breeze
with flowing robes, and points her toes daintily:
another walks like the wife of a red-faced Umbrian,
feet wide apart, and with **huge** paces.
But there's measure here as in most **things**: both the rustic's stride,
and the more affected step should be foregone.
Still, let the parts of your lower shoulder and upper arm
on the left side, be naked, to be admired.
That suits **you** pale-skinned girls especially: when I see it,
I want to kiss **you**r shoulder, as far as it's shown.

BOOK III PART VII: LEARN MUSIC AND READ THE POETS

The Sirens were sea-monsters, who, with singing voice,
could restrain a ship's course as they wished.
Ulysses, your body nearly melted hearing them,
while the wax filled your companions' ears.
Song is a thing of grace: girls, learn **to** sing:
for many your voice is a better procuress than your looks.
And repeat what you just heard in the marble theatre,
and the latest songs played in the Egyptian style.
No woman taught under my control should fail to know
how to hold her lyre with the left hand, the plectrum with her right.
Thracian Orpheus, with his lute, moved animals and stones,
and Tartarus's lake and Cerberus, the triple-headed hound.
At your song, Amphion, just **avenge**r of **your mother**,
the stones obligingly made Thebes's new walls.
Though dumb, a Dolphin's thought to have responded
to a human voice, as the tale of Arion's lyre noted.
And learn to sweep both hands across the genial harp
that too is suitable for our sweet fun.
Let Callimachus, be known to you, Coan Philetas
and the Teian Muse of old drunken Anacreon:
And let Sappho be yours (well what's more wanton?),
Menander, whose master's gulled by his Thracian slaves' cunning.
and be able to recite tender Propertius's song,
or some of yours Gallus or Tibullus:
and the high-flown speech of Varro's fleece
of golden wool, Phrixus, your sister Helle's lament:
and Aeneas the wanderer, the beginnings of mighty Rome,
than which there is no better known work in Latin.
And perhaps my name will be mingled with those,
my works not all given to Lethe's streams:

and someone will say: 'Read our master's cultured song,
in which he teaches both the sexes: or choose
from the three books stamped with the title Amores,
that you recite softly with sweetly-teachable lips:
or let your voice sing those letters he composed, the Heroides:
he **invent**ed that form unknown to others.'
O grant it so, Phoebus! And, you, sacred powers of poetry,
great horned Bacchus, and the Nine goddesses!

BOOK III PART VIII: LEARN DANCING, GAMES

Who doubts I'd wish **a girl** to know how to dance,
and move her limbs as decreed when the wine goes round?
The body's artistes, the theatre's spectacle, are loved:
so great's the gracefulness of their agility.
A few things shameful to mention, she must know how to call
the throws at knucklebones, and your values, you rolled dice:
sometimes throwing three, sometimes thinking, closely,
how to advance craftily, how to challenge.
She should play the chess match warily not rashly,
where one piece can be lost to two opponents,
and a warrior wars without his companion who's been taken,
and a rival often has to retrace the journey he began.
Light spills should be poured from the open bag,
nor should a spill be disturbed unless she can raise it.
There's a kind of game, the board squared-off by as many lines,
with precise calculation, as the fleeting year has months:
a smaller board presents three stones each on either side
where the winner will have made his line up together.
There's **a** thousand games to be had: it's shameful for a girl
not to know how to play: playing often brings on love.
But there's not much labour in knowing all the moves:
there's much more work in keeping to your rules.
We're **reckless**, and revealed by eagerness itself,
and in a game the naked **heart**'s exposed:
Anger enters, ugly mischief, desire for gain,
quarrels and fights and anxious pain:
accusations fly, the air echoes with shouts,
and each calls on their outraged deities:
there's no honour, they seek to cancel their debts at whim:
and often I've seen cheeks wet with tears.

Jupiter keep you **free** from all such vile reproaches,
you who have any anxiety to please men.

BOOK III PART IX: BE SEEN AROUND

Idle Nature has allotted these games to girls:
men have more opportunity to play.
Theirs the swift ball, the javelin and the hoop,
and arms, and horses made to go in a circle.
You have no Field of Mars, no ice-cold Aqua Virgo,
you don't swim in the Tiber's calm waters.
But it's fine to be seen out walking in the shade of Pompey's
Porch when your head's on fire with Virgo's heavenly horses:
visit the holy Palatine of laurel-wreathed Phoebus:
he sank Cleopatra's galleys in the deep:
the arcades Livia, Caesar's wife, and his sister, Octavia, started,
and his son-in-law Agrippa's, crowned with naval honours:
visit the incense-smoking altars of the Egyptian heifer,
visit the three theatres, take some conspicuous seat:
let the sand that's drenched with warm blood be seen,
and the impetuous wheels rounding the turning-post.
What's hidden is unknown: nothing unknown's desired:
there's no prize for a face that truly lacks a witness.
Though you excel Thamyras and Amoebeus in song,
there's no great applause for an unknown lyre.
If Apelles of Cos had never sculpted Venus,
she'd be hidden, sunk beneath the waters.
What do sacred poets seek but fame?
It's the final goal of all our labours.
Poets were once the concern of gods and kings:
and the ancient chorus earned a big reward.
A bard's dignity was inviolable: his name was honoured,
and he was often granted vast wealth.
Ennius earned it, born in Calabria's hills,
buried next to you, great Scipio.

Now the ivy wreaths lie without honour, and the painful toil
of the learned Muses, in the night, has the name of idleness.
But he's delighted to stay awake for fame: who'd know Homer,
if his immortal work the Iliad were unknown?
Who'd know of Danae, if she'd always been imprisoned,
and lay hidden, an old woman, **in her tower**?
Lovely girls, the crowd is useful to you.
Often lift your feet above the threshold.
The wolf shadows many sheep, to snatch just one,
and Jupiter's eagle stoops on many birds.
So too a lovely woman must let the people see her:
and perhaps there'll be one among them she attracts.
Keen to please she'll linger in all those places,
and apply her whole mind to caring for her beauty.
Chance rules everywhere: always dangle your bait:
the fish will lurk in the least likely pool.
Often hounds wander the wooded hills in vain,
and the deer, un-driven, walks into the net.
What was less hoped for by Andromeda, in chains,
than that her tears could please anyone?
Often a lover's found at a husband's funeral: walking
with loosened hair and unchecked weeping suits you.

BOOK III PART X: BEWARE OF FALSE LOVERS

Avoid those men who profess to looks and culture,
who keep their hair carefully in place.
What they tell you they've told a thousand girls:
their love wanders and lingers in no one place.
Woman, what can you do with a man more delicate than you,
and one perhaps who has more lovers too?
You'll scarcely credit it, but credit this: Troy would remain,
if Cassandra's warnings had been heeded.
Some will attack you with a lying pretence of love,
and through that opening seek a shameful gain.
But don't be tricked by hair gleaming with liquid nard,
or short tongues pressed into their creases:
don't be ensnared by a toga of finest threads,
or that there's a ring on every finger.
Perhaps the **be**st dressed among them all's **a thief,**
and burns with love of your finery.
'Give it me back!' the girl who's robbed will often cry,
'Give it me back!' at the top of her voice in the cattle-market.
Venus, from your temple, all glittering with gold,
you calmly watch the quarrel, and you, Appian nymphs.
There are names known for a certain sort of reputation too,
they're guilty of deceiving many lovers.
Learn from other's grief to fear your own:
don't let the door be opened to lying men.
Athenian girls, beware of trusting Theseus's oaths:
those gods he calls to witness, he's called on before.
And you, Demophoon, heir to Theseus's crimes,
no honour remains to you, with Phyllis left behind.
If they promise truly, promise in as many words:
and if they give, you give the joys that were agreed.

She might as well put out the sleepless Vestal's fire,
and **snatch** the holy relics from your Temple, Ino,
and give her man hemlock and monkshood crushed together,
as deny him sex if she's received his gifts.

BOOK III PART XI: TAKE CARE WITH LETTERS

Let me speak closer to the theme: hold the reins,
Muses, don't smash the wheels with galloping.
His letters written on fir-wood tablets test the waters:
make sure a suitable servant receives the message.
Consider it: and read what, gathered from his own words, he said,
and perhaps, from its intent, what he might anxiously be asking.
And wait a little while before you answer: waiting
always arouses love, if it's only for a short **time**.
But don't give in too easily to a young man's prayers,
nor yet deny him what he seeks out of cruelty.
Make him fear and hope together, **every time you write,**
let hope seem more certain and fear grow less.
Write elegantly girls, but in neutral ordinary words,
an everyday sort of style pleases:
Ah! How often a doubting lover's been **set** on **fire** by letters,
and good looks have been harmed by barbarous words!
But since, though you lack the marriage ribbons,
it's your concern to deceive your lovers,
write the tablets in your maid's or boy's hand,
don't trust these tokens **to** a new young man.
He who keeps such tokens is treacherous,
but nevertheless he holds the flames of Etna.
I've seen girls, made pallid by this terror,
submit to slavery, poor things, for many years.
I judge that countering fraud with fraud's allowed,
the law lets arms be wielded against arms.
One form's used in exercising many hands,
(Ah! Perish those that give me reason for this warning)
don't write again on wax unless it's all been scraped,
lest the single tablet contain two hands.

And always speak of your lover as female when you write:
let it be 'her' in **your** letters, instead of 'him'.

BOOK III PART XII: AVOID THE VICES, FAVOUR THE POETS

If I might turn from lesser to greater things,
and spread the full expanse of swelling sail,
it's important to banish looks of anger from your face:
bright peace suits human beings, anger the wild beast.
Anger swells the face: the veins darken with blood:
the eyes flash more savagely than the Gorgon's.
'Away with you, flute, you're not worth all that,'
said Pallas when she saw her face in the water.
You too if you looked in the mirror in your anger,
that girl would scarcely know her own face.
Pride does no less harm to your looks:
love is attracted to friendly eyes.
We hate (believe the expert) extravagant disdain:
a silent face often sows the seeds of our dislike.
Glance at a glance, smile tenderly at a smile:
he nods, you too return the signal you received.
When he's practised, so, the boy leaves the foils,
and takes his sharp **arrows** from his quiver.
We hate sad girls too: let Ajax choose Tecmessa:
a happy girl charms us cheerful people.
I'd never ask you, Andromache, or you, Tecmessa
while there's another lover for me than you.
I find it hard to believe, though I'm forced to by your children,
that you ever slept with your husbands.
Do you suppose that gloomy wife ever said to Ajax:
'Light of my life': or the words that usually delight a man?
Who'll prevent me using great examples for little things,
why should we be afraid **of** the leader's name?
Our good leader trusts those commanders with a squad,
these with the cavalry, that man to guard the standard:

You too should judge what each of us is good for,
and place each one in his proper role.
The rich give gifts: the lawyer appears as promised:
often he pleads a client's case that must be heard:
We who make songs, can only send you songs:
we are the choir here best suited above all to love.
We can make beauties that please us widely known:
Nemesis has a name, and Cynthia has:
you'll have heard of Lycoris from East to West:
and many ask who my Corinna is.
Add that guile is absent from the sacred poets,
and our art too fashions our characters.
Ambition and **desire** for possession don't touch us:
the shady couch is cherished, the forum scorned.
But we're easily caught, torn by powerful passions,
and we know too well how to love with perfect faith.
No doubt our minds are sweetened by gentle art,
and our natures are consistent with our studies.
Girls, **be** kind to the poets of Helicon:
there's divinity in them, and they're the Muses' friends.
There's a god in us, and our dealings are with the heavens:
this inspiration comes from ethereal heights.
It's a sin to hope for gifts from the poet:
ah me! No girl's afraid of that sin.
Still hide it, don't look **greedy** at first sight:
new love will balk when it sees the snare.

BOOK III PART XIII: TRY YOUNG AND OLDER LOVERS

No rider rules a horse that's lately known the reins,
with the same bit as one that's truly mastered,
nor will the same way serve to captivate
the mind of mature years and of green youth.
This raw recruit, first known of now in love's campaigns,
who reaches your threshold, a fresh prize,
must know you only, always cling to you alone:
this crop must be surrounded by high hedges.
Keep rivals away: you'll win while you hold just one:
love and power don't last long when they're shared.
Your older warrior loves sensibly and wisely,
suffers much that the beginner won't endure:
he won't break the door down, **burn** it with cruel fire,
attack his mistress's tender cheeks with his nails,
or rip apart his clothing or his girl's,
nor will torn hair be a cause of tears.
That suits hot boys, the time of strong desire:
but he'll bear cruel wounds with calm mind.
He burns, alas, with slow fires, like wet straw,
like new-cut timber on the mountain height.
This love's more sure: that's brief and more prolific:
snatch the swift fruits, that fly, in your hand.

BOOK III PART XIV: USE **JEALOUS**Y AND FEAR

Let all be betrayed: I've unbarred the gates to the enemy:
and let my loyalty be to treacherous betrayal.
What's easily given nourishes love poorly:
mingle the odd rejection with welcome fun.
Let him lie before the door, crying: 'Cruel entrance!',
pleading very humbly, threatening a lot too.
We can't stand sweetness: bitterness renews our taste:
often a yacht sinks swamped by a favourable wind:
this is what bitter wives can't endure:
their husbands can come to them when they wish:
add a closed door and a hard-mouthed janitor,
saying: 'You can't,' and love will touch you too.
Drop the blunted foils now: fight with blades:
no doubt I'll be attacked with my own weapons.
Also when the lover you've just caught falls into the net,
let him think that only he has access to your room.
Later let him sense a rival, the bed's shared pact:
remove these arts, and love grows old.
The horse runs swiftly from the **star**ting gate,
when he has others to pass, and others follow.
Wrongs relight the dying fires, as you wish:
See (I confess!), I don't love unless I'm hurt.
Still, don't give cause for grief, excessively,
let the anxious man suspect it, rather than know.
Stir him with a dismal watchman, fictitiously set to guard you,
and the excessively irksome care of a harsh husband.
Pleasure that comes with safety's less enjoyable:
though you're freer than Thais, pretend fear.
Though the door's easier, let him in at the window,
and show signs of fear on your face.

A clever maid should leap up and cry: 'We're lost!'
You, **hide** the trembling youth in any hole.
Still safe loving should be mixed with fright,
lest he consider you hardly worth a night.

BOOK III PART XV: PLAY CLOAK AND DAGGER

I nearly forgot the skilful ways by which you can
elude a husband, or a vigilant guardian.
let the bride fear her husband: to guard a wife is right:
it's fitting, it's decreed by law, the courts, and modesty.
But for you too be guarded, scarcely released from prison,
who could bear it? Adhere to my religion, and deceive!
Though as many eyes as Argus owned observe you,
you'll deceive them (if only your will is firm).
How can a guard make sure that you can't write,
when you're given all that time to spend washing?
When a knowing maid can carry letters you've penned,
concealed in the deep curves of her warm breasts?
When she can hide papers fastened to her calf,
or bear charming notes tied beneath her feet?
The guard's on the look-out for that, your go-between
offers her back as paper, and takes your words on her flesh.
Also a letter's safe, and deceives the eye, written with fresh milk;
you read it by scattering it with crushed ashes.
And those traced out with a point wetted with linseed oil,
so that **the** empty tablet carries **secret** messages.
Acrisius took care to imprison his daughter, Danae:
but she still made him a grandfather by her sin.
What good's a guard, with so many theatres in the city,
when she's free to gaze at horses paired together,
when she sits occupied with the Egyptian heifer's sistrum,
and goes where male companions cannot go,
when male eyes are banned from Bona Dea's temple,
except those she orders to enter?
When, with the girls' clothes guarded by a servant at the door,
the baths conceal so many secret joys,

when, however many times she's needed, a friend feigns illness,
and however ill she is can leave her bed,
when the false **key** tells **by** its name what we should do,
and the door alone doesn't grant the exits you seek?
And the jailor's attention's fuddled with much wine,
even though the grapes were picked on Spanish hills:
then there are drugs that bring deep sleep,
and close eyes overcome by Lethe's night:
or your maid can rightly detain the wretch with lengthy games,
and be associated herself with long delays.
but why use these tortuous ways and minor rules,
when the least gift will buy a guardian?
Believe me gifts captivate men and gods:
Jupiter himself is pleased with the gifts he's given.
What can the wise man do, when the fool loves gifts?
He'll be silent too when a gift's accepted.
But let the guard be bought for once and all:
who surrenders to it once, will surrender often.
I remember I lamented, friends are to be feared:
that complaint's not only true of men.
If you're credulous, others snatch your joys,
and that hare you started running goes to others.
She too, who eagerly offers room and bed,
believe me, she's been mine more than once.
Don't let too beautiful a maid serve you:
she's often offered herself to me as my lady.

BOOK III PART XVI: MAKE HIM BELIEVE HE'S LOVED

What am I talking of, madman? Why show a naked front
to the enemy, and betray myself on my own evidence?
The bird doesn't show the hunter where to find it,
the stag doesn't teach the savage hounds to run.
Let others seek advantage: faithful to how I started, I'll go on:
I'll give the Lemnian girls swords to kill me.
Make us believe (it's so easy) that we're loved:
faith comes easily to the loving in their prayers.
let a woman look longingly at her young man, sigh deeply,
and ask him why he comes so late:
add tears, and feigned grief over a rival,
and tear at his cheeks with her nails:
he'll straight away be convinced: and she'll be pitied,
and he'll say: 'She's seized by love of me.'
Especially if he's cultured, pleased with his mirror,
he'll believe he could touch the goddesses with love.
But you, whatever wrong occurs, be lightly troubled,
nor in poor spirits if you hear of a rival.
Don't believe too quickly: how quick belief can wound,
Procris should be an example to you.
There's a sacred fountain, and sweet green-turfed ground,
near to the bright slopes of flowered Hymettus:
the low woods form a grove: **strawberry-trees** touch the grass,
it smells of rosemary, bay and black myrtle:
there's no lack of foliage, dense box and fragile tamarisk,
nor fine clover, and cultivated pine.
The many kinds of leaves and grass-heads tremble
at the touch of light winds and refreshing breezes.
The quiet pleased Cephalus: leaving men and dogs **behind**,
the weary youth often settled on this spot,

'Come, fickle breeze (Aura), who cools my heat'
he used to sing, 'be welcome to my breast.'
Some officious person, evilly remembering what he'd heard,
brought it to the wife's fearful hearing:
Procris, as she took the name Aura to be some rival,
fainted, and was suddenly dumb with grief:
She grew pale, as the leaves of choice vine-stalks
grow pale, wounded by an early winter,
or ripe quinces arching on their branches,
or cornelian cherries not yet fit for us to eat.
As her breath returned, she tore the thin clothing from her breast,
and scratched at her innocent cheeks with her nails:
Then she fled quickly, frenzied, down the ways,
hair flowing, like a Maenad roused by the thyrsus.
As she came near, she left her companions in the valley,
bravely herself entered the grove, in secret, on silent feet.
What was in your mind, when you hid there so foolishly,
Procris? What ardour, in **your** terrified **heart**?
Did you think she'd come soon, Aura, whoever she was,
and her infamy be visible to your eyes.
Now regretting that you came (not wishing to surprise them)
now pleased: doubting love twists at your heart.
The place, the name, the witness, command belief,
and the mind always thinks what it fears is true.
She saw signs that a body had pressed down the grass,
her chest throbbed, quivering with its anxious heart.
Now noon had contracted the thin shadows,
and dawn and twilight were parted equally:
behold, Cephalus, Hermes's child, re**turn**ed to the wood,
and plunged his burning face in the fountain's water.
You hid, Procris, anxiously: he lay down as usual on the grass,
and cried: 'Come you zephyrs, you sweet air (Aura)!'
As her joyous error in the name came to the miserable girl,
her wits and the true colour of her face returned.
She rose, and **with** agitated body moved **the** opposing leaves,

a wife running to her husband's arms:
He, sure a wild beast moved, leapt youthfully to his feet,
grasping his spear in his right hand.
What are you doing, unhappy man? That's no creature,
hold back your throw! Alas, your girl's pierced by your spear!
She called out: 'Ah me! You've pierced a loving heart.
That part always takes its wound from Cephalus.
I die before my time, but not wounded by a rival:
that will ensure you, **earth**, lie lightly on me.
Now my spirit departs into that air with its deceptive name:
I pass, I go, dear hand, close my eyes!'
He held the body of his dying lady on his sad breast,
and bathed the cruel wound with his tears.
She died, and her breath, passing little by little
from her rash breast, was caught on her sad lover's lips.

BOOK III PART XVII: WATCH HOW YOU EAT AND DRINK

But to resume the work: bare facts for me
so that my weary vessel can reach harbour.
You're anxiously expecting, while I lead you to dinner,
that you can even ask for my advice there too.
Come late, and come upon us charmingly in the lamplight:
you'll come with pleasing delay: delay's a grand seductress.
Even if you're plain, with drink you'll seem beautiful,
and night itself grants concealment to your failings.
Take the food daintily: how you eat does matter:
don't smear your face all over with a greasy hand.
Don't eat before at home, but stop before you're full:
be a little less eager than you can be:
if Paris, Priam's son, saw ·Helen eating greedily,
he'd detest it, and say: 'Mine's a foolish prize.'
It's more fitting, and it suits girls more, to drink:
Bacchus you don't go badly with Venus's boy.
So long as the head holds out, and the mind **and** feet
stand firm: and you don't see two of what's only one.
Shameful a woman lying there, drenched with too much wine:
she's worthy of sleeping with anyone who'll have her.
And it's not safe to fall asleep at table:
many shameful things usually happen in sleep.

BOOK III PART XVIII: AND SO TO BED

To have been taught more is shameful: but kindly Venus
said: 'What's shameful is my particular concern.'
Let each girl know herself: adopt a reliable posture
for her body: one layout's not suitable for all.
She who's known for her face, lie there face upwards:
let her back be seen, she who's back delights.
Milanion bore Atalanta's legs on his shoulders:
if they're good looking, that mode's acceptable.
Let the small be carried by a horse: Andromache,
his Theban bride, was too tall to straddle Hector's horse.
Let a woman noted for her length of body,
press the bed with her knees, arch her neck slightly.
She who has youthful thighs, and faultless breasts,
the man might stand, she spread, with her body downwards.
Don't think it shameful to loosen your hair, like a Maenad,
and throw back your head with its flowing tresses.
You too, whom Lucina's marked with childbirth's wrinkles,
like the swift child of Parthia, turn your mount around.
There's a thousand ways to do it: simple and least effort,
is just to lie there half-turned on your right side.
But neither Phoebus's tripods nor Ammon's horn
shall **sing** greater truths to you than my Muse:
If you trust art's promise, that I've long employed:
my songs will offer you their promise.
Woman, feel love, melted to your very bones,
and let both delight equally in the thing.
Don't leave out seductive coos and delightful murmurings,
don't let wild words be silent in the middle of your games.
You too whom nature denies sexual feeling,
pretend to sweet delight with artful sounds.

Unhappy girl, for whom that sluggish place is numb,
which man and woman equally should enjoy.
Only beware when you feign it, lest it shows:
create belief in your movements and your eyes.
When you **like** it, show it with cries and panting breath:
Ah! I blush, that part has its own secret signs.
She who asks fondly for **a** gift after love's delights,
can't want her request to carry any weight.
Don't let light into the room through all the windows:
it's fitting for much of your body to be concealed.

The game is done: time to descend, you swans,
you who bent your necks beneath my yoke.
As once the boys, so now my crowd of **girl**s
inscribe on your trophies 'Ovid was my master.'

how to be a poet:

come as a dark star. catch the sun
in your one mouth. be trouble. be the girl
who is too beautiful. need nothing. become
a city. be un–boy-like, a willing
song. if you can, lay there in the light.
enumerate water. set your nets to cicadas
in summer. with unpractised hands,
seek out delight. hesitate
like ice. hold fast to the fish
on the hook. hollow the ocean. kiss
the imaginary mouth. bring a promise
like an apple in the hand. speak
as if you were stone. go wildly
in the woods unhearing
many secret things, confessing
excessive love in the fields
of the body. take what
isn't given. hope for the honey.

follow the sea with salt–green
lips. hold violets and open
lilies. demand gentleness. whatever
engenders surrender. remember
everything. lie there on the open roof. chase
the heart of your reader
and your loveliest rival. gather
absence. cultivate your sorrow
garden. those seeds are swollen
with brightness. allow
your happiness. be seen.

carry sea-shells in the night, believe
me, even if you never
believed. grow a thousand
eyes, then wait. this is the work.
come to the tender pen.

beware of the many warnings
from your girlhood. for example,
be afraid. be stubborn
as the sky's colour, decisive
as teeth. forbid your smallness
and seek huge things
that suit you. i want you to
avenge your mother. invent
a girl with a reckless heart.
free her in her tower. be a thief,
snatch time, every time you write,
set fire to your arrows
of desire. be greedy, burn
like a jealous star. hide the secret key
by the strawberry-trees behind
your heart. turn with the earth
and sing like a girl.

Andrews McMeel Publishing
a division of Andrews McMeel Universal
1130 Walnut Street, Kansas City, Missouri 64106

www.andrewsmcmeel.com

19 20 21 22 23 SDB 10 9 8 7 6 5 4 3 2 1

ISBN: 978-1-4494-9554-1

Library of Congress Control Number: 2019940629

From *Ovid: The Love Poems* by A. S. Kline TRANSLATOR, Copyright © 2001

Editor: Patty Rice
Art Director/Designer: Holly Swayne
Production Editor: Elizabeth A. Garcia
Production Manager: Cliff Koehler